MW00946504

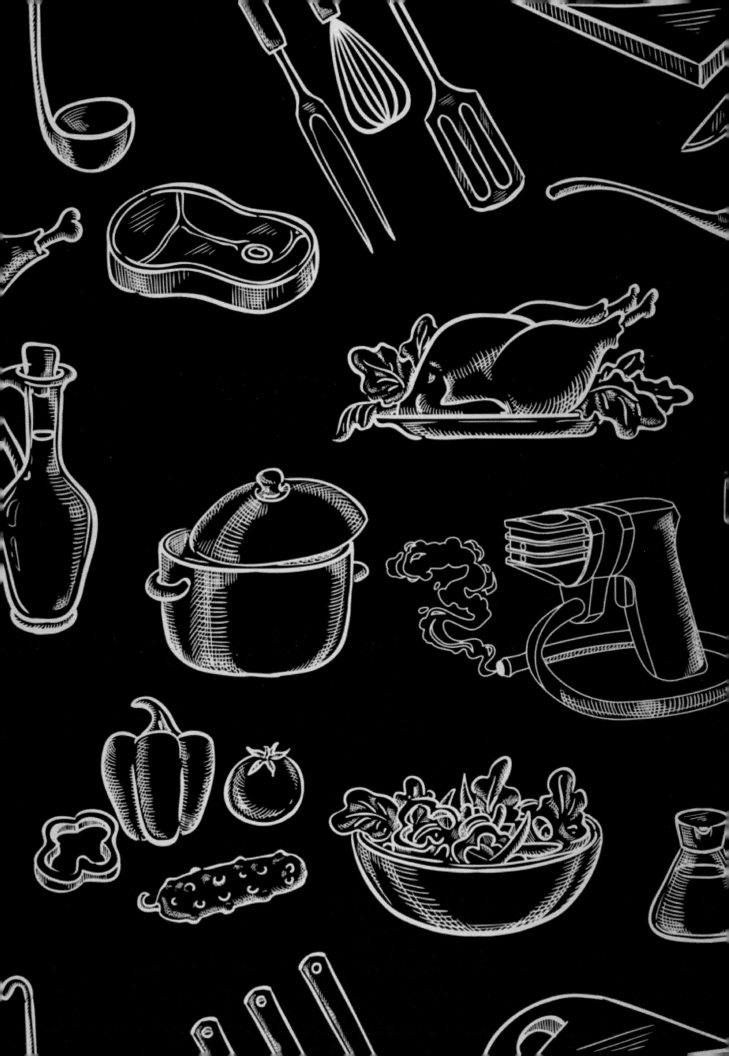

Copyright © 2010 by Homia

All rights reserved. This book or any portion thereof

may not be reproduced or used in any manner whatsoever

without the express written permission of the publisher

except for the use of brief quotations in a book review.

Printed in the United States of America

First Printing, 2022

ISBN 9798358122598

www.homia.us

homia

THE ART OF SMOKE

SMOKING GUN FOOD RECIPES (BONUS 5 SMOKED COCKTAILS)

JOSS LINDE

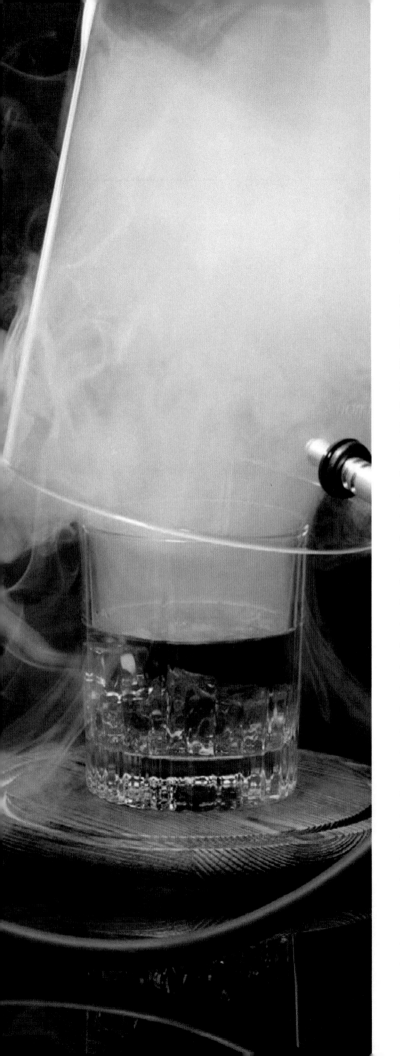

CONTENTS

INTRODUCTION

Are you an avid appreciator of delicious and unforgettable meals? Do you find yourself struggling with time-consuming, expensive, and tedious preparation? We feel your pain and are ready to help! We are making your favorite cookouts extra special and stress-free by providing these delicious recipes in our new book, "Smoking gun Recipes." From a variety of meets, cooked in different styles, seafood from all around the world, and gourmet dishes, built from delicious ingredients - it doesn't stop there either! As you prepare your unique meals with this book, the best thing is waiting for you in the end - breathtaking desserts. There is something for every part of the day, every occasion, and every taste. As you explore your inner chef through every page, you will be fascinated by the variety of classic barbeque favorites, sophisticated sauces, specialty dishes, side dishes, and desserts. You'll find plenty more favorites like this in addition to learning how easy they can be made using only one tool: The Smoking Gun Of course. Smoking gun is one of the best innovations in the culinary world, as it has made smoked meals a comfort food.

However, every professional cook needs some guidance in the begging. The smoking Gun recipe book offers detailed instructions and tips obtained from years of experience in smoked meals. Whether you are a stranger in the kitchen or consider it your second home, clear step-by-step instructions will lead you to the path of success in everything you decide to smoke. Nearly 100 recipes are equipped with full-color photos, shopping suggestions, and the author's secret tips and tricks. This essential cookbook is a game-changer for smoking gun owners who want to get a restaurant quality and experience without expert help. But what can make a fantastic meal even better? If you said "an equally amazing cocktail", you are correct! We have included 5 fan-favorite smoked cocktail recipes to put a cherry on top of your meal. Already ready to start? Enjoy your magical smoking experience and we will see you on the next page!

ABOUT THE AUTHOR

Joss is a German food photographer, born in Germany, raised in Belgium, and currently living in Thailand.

He is not just a photographer, but also a chef who takes his guests on a new journey into the world of food. Joss worked as a chef for almost 10 years on several stations in Berlin, Cambodia, and Thailand, which gave him a profound understanding of different cuisines, dishes, and food characteristics.

The pairing of his skills as a chef and his knowledge in the culinary field makes him passionate to combine food with photography. After his start as an independent food photographer, Joss soon developed his very own style, which is defined by airy, light photographs with natural lighting, seasonal ingredients, and a love for details. His food photographs are mouthwatering and can turn simple dishes into fabulous creations. For him, not only the food is important, but also the styling and setting of each ingredient. He prepares all of the dishes he photographs himself.

Fascinated by the flavors of asian cuisine he decided to move to Thailand and train in award-winning restaurants to learn techniques of innovative Thai cuisine. Since then Joss traveled throughout Asia to discover the Taste of Asian Food and satisfy his desire to experience the world of Asian flavors.

HOW TO USE A SMOKING GUN

A SMOKING GUN IS VERY EASY TO USE.

1. First, choose the food you want to smoke and prepare the container you want to use to trap the smoke. Common choices are cloche or plastic wrap. Insert the end of the smoking gun, the hose, into the container.

2. Fill the smoking chamber of your smoking gun with your favorite wood chips, then turn on the machine.

3. Light the wood chips. The fan inside the smoking gun will blow air through the wood chips and generate smoke.

4. Fill your container with smoke then remove the hose, leaving the container fully closed.

5. Leave the smoke enclosed in the container for a specific amount of time. The length of time depends on how much smoke flavor you want.

6. Remove the Container and release the smoke.

7. Enjoy your smoky-flavored food!

TIPS

- There are a few steps to learn before using the smoking gun, to find the balance between smoke and time:

  - If you want a light smoke flavor, 3 minutes of smoking time is enough.
  - For a more intense flavor, smoke your food for 5-10 minutes. It all depends on your personal preference.

- Feel free to experiment with different smoke flavors and your favorite food or drink.

- Choose your favorite wood chips and learn which smoking wood types and flavors are the best for each dish you are smoking. One of my favorite wood chips is hickory, apple, and cherry wood. Hickory Wood chips give a smoky bacon-like flavor which works well with pork or ribs. Apple and Cherry wood chips produce a sweet fruity flavor which goes well with poultry, and fish but also with desserts and sweet cocktails. These are just some examples, **feel free to experiment**.

SNACKS

SMOKED SWEET POTATO FRIES

INGREDIENTS

- 1 large sweet potato
- pinch of sea salt
- pinch of black pepper
- ½ tsp garlic powder
- 1 tbsp parsley, chopped
- ½ lemon, sliced
- cooking oil
- oak wood chips

Prep Time	10 Min.
Cooking Time	20 Min.
Smoking Time	5-10 Min.
Portion	2
Category	SNACK

INSTRUCTIONS

⚜ Preheat the oven to 375 °F.

⚜ Peel and cut the sweet potato into sticks.
Toss the sweet potato sticks in the oil with salt, pepper and garlic powder.
Line a baking sheet with baking paper and place the sweet potato sticks on it.
Bake for 10 min then flip and bake for another 10 minutes until golden brown.

⚜ Remove from the oven and cover with the lid.
Fill the smoking chamber of the gun with the oak wood chips and light it.
Place the nose under the lid and fill with smoke.
Let the sweet potato fries infuse with smoke for 5-10 minutes.

⚜ Remove the lid and serve the fries with lemon slices and fresh parsley!

SMOKED VEGETARIAN SPRING ROLLS

INGREDIENTS

- 12 pieces spring roll dough
- 2 tbsp sunflower oil
- red onion, diced
- 1 carrot, shredded
- 1 clove garlic, minced
- 5 cups cabbage, shredded
- pinch of salt
- 1 tbsp soy sauce
- ½ tbsp sesame seeds
- apple wood chips

Prep Time	10 Min.
Cooking Time	30 Min.
Smoking Time	3-5 Min.
Portion	12 rolls
Category	SNACK

INSTRUCTIONS

- Heat a large pan over medium high heat. Add the oil then saute the onions and garlic. Add in the vegetables.

- Once the vegetables are tender, season with soy sauce and salt then remove from the pan and set aside. Sprinkle with the sesame seeds.

- Lay one piece of spring roll dough on a clean surface. Place 2 tbsp of filling on the bottom of each spring roll dough. Slowly roll to the top then fold the sides to close the spring roll. Seal the edges with water. Brush the rolls with some oil, then bake in the oven for 20 minutes at 360 °F until crispy. Transfer the spring rolls to a plate.

- Cover the plate with plastic wrap and place the hose of the smoking gun inside. Fill the smoking chamber with the apple wood chips. Turn on the smoking gun and light the chips.

- Infuse the spring rolls with the smoke for at least 3-5 minutes.

  Remove the lid and serve the spring rolls warm!

SMOKED SAUSAGE PUFFS

INGREDIENTS

- 5 pieces Puff Pastry
- 5 sausages
- 1 egg
- ½ cup pickled cucumbers
- hickory wood chips

Prep Time	10 Min.
Cooking Time	20 Min.
Smoking Time	5-10 Min.
Portion	2
Category	SNACK

INSTRUCTIONS

☘ Preheat the oven to 360 °F.

☘ Roll the puff pastry sheets out on a floured surface and cut into the rectangles of the same length as the sausages.

☘ Place each sausage along each pastry strip.

☘ Beat 1 egg in a small bowl. Brush one end of the pastry with the beaten egg and roll the sausage up in the pastry, sealing the ends.

☘ Chill the sausage pastry in the fridge for 5 minutes.

☘ Remove from the fridge and brush each sausage roll with the beaten egg. Bake in the oven for 20 minutes until the pastry is golden brown.

☘ Remove from the oven and cover with plastic wrap. Fill the smoking chamber of the gun with the hickory wood chips. Place the rubber hose under the wrap to allow smoke to fill the bowl. Cover the bowl completely to prevent the smoke from escaping.

☘ Turn on the smoking gun and light the wood with a lighter. Once the bowl is completely filled with smoke remove the rubber hose and cover the bowl again.

☘ Infuse the sausage rolls with the smoke for at least 5-10 minutes. Remove the plastic wrap and serve the sausage rolls!

SMOKED MEDITERRANEAN CHICKPEA SALAD

INGREDIENTS

- 2 cans chick peas
- 1 cup red onions, chopped
- 1 cup cucumber, diced
- 1 cup cherry tomatoes, halved
- 1 lemon, juice
- 2 tbsp extra virgin olive oil
- ½ cup parsley, chopped
- pinch of sea salt and black pepper
- pear wood chips

Prep Time	10 Min.
Smoking Time	3-5 Min.
Portion	4
Category	SNACK

INSTRUCTIONS

🌿 Drain and rinse the chickpeas.

Place the chickpeas in a bowl together with the cucumbers, tomatoes, red onions and parsley.

Combine the lemon juice and olive oil.

Pour the dressing over the salad and season with salt and pepper.

Mix well.

🌿 Transfer to a bowl and cover with plastic wrap.

Add the pear wood chips to the smoking chamber of the smoking gun and place the hose under the plastic wrap.

Light the wood chips and fill the jar with smoke.

Close the jar and let the smoke infuse the chickpea salad for 3-5 minutes.

🌿 Open the lid or wrap and serve the smoked chickpea salad.

SMOKED MASH POTATOES

INGREDIENTS

- 35 oz. potatoes
- ¼ cup milk
- 4 tbsp butter
- pinch of salt
- pinch of nutmeg powder
- cotton wood chips

Prep Time	15 Min.
Smoking Time	5-10 Min.
Portion	4
Category	SNACK

INSTRUCTIONS

⚜ Get the smoking gun ready and fill with the cotton wood chips.

⚜ Prepare all the ingredients.

Peel the potatoes, cut them into dices and cook in boiling water until cooked.

Press the cooked potatoes through a potato press.

Bring the milk to a boil and add the mashed potatoes.

Season with salt and nutmeg.

⚜ Cover the bowl with plastic wrap.

Place the rubber hose of the smoking gun under the wrap to allow smoke to fill the bowl.

Cover the bowl completely to prevent the smoke from escaping.

⚜ Turn on the smoking gun and light the wood chips with a lighter.

Once the bowl is completely filled with smoke remove the rubber hose and cover the bowl again.

⚜ Infuse the mashed potatoes with the smoke for at least 5-10 minutes.

Remove the plastic wrap and serve the mashed potatoes as a side dish!

SMOKED CAPRESE SKEWERS

INGREDIENTS

- ½ bunch of fresh basil
- 12 cherry tomatoes
- 12 fresh mozzarella balls
- extra virgin olive oil
- salt and pepper
- cherry wood chips

Prep Time	10 Min.
Smoking Time	3-5 Min.
Portion	2
Category	SNACK

INSTRUCTIONS

Place cherry tomatoes and mozzarella on each wooden stick.

Arrange the skewers on a plate, season with salt and pepper, drizzle with the olive oil.

Garnish each skewer with basil leaves.

Place a lid over the plate and place the hose under the lid.

Fill the smoking chamber with the cherry wood chips.

Turn on the smoking gun and light the chips.

Infuse the caprese skewers with the smoke for 3-5 minutes.

Remove the lid and serve the caprese skewers!

SMOKED BASIL PESTO

INGREDIENTS

- 2 cups fresh italian basil
- ½ cup parmesan, grated
- 2 cloves garlic
- ½ cup extra virgin olive oil
- pinch salt and pepper
- ¼ cup walnuts
- pecan wood chips

Prep Time	5 Min.
Smoking Time	5-10 Min.
Portion	1 jar
Category	SNACK

INSTRUCTIONS

- In a small bowl combine the basil leaves, parmesan cheese, walnuts, garlic, salt and pepper in a food processor. Pulse until coarsely chopped.

  Continue to blend, slowly adding the olive oil until desired consistency.

  Transfer the basil pesto into a jar.

- Place the hose under the lid of the jar.

  Fill the smoking chamber with the pecan wood chips.

  Turn on the smoking gun and light the chips.

- Infuse the basil pesto with the smoke for at least 5-10 minutes.

  Remove the lid and serve the basil pesto!

SMOKED BAKED FALAFEL

INGREDIENTS

- 16 oz dried chickpeas, canned
- 1 small onion, diced
- 1 clove garlic, minced
- 2 tsp cumin
- ¼ tsp cayenne pepper
- juice of ½ lemon
- ¼ cup chickpea flour
- pinch of salt and black pepper
- 2 tbsp tahini paste
- ½ bunch fresh cilantro
- ½ cup cherry tomatoes, halved
- ¼ cup cucumber, diced
- hickory wood chips

Prep Time	10 Min.
Smoking Time	3-8 Min.
Portion	4
Category	SNACK

INSTRUCTIONS

⚜ Preheat the oven to 390 °F.

⚜ Place the soaked chickpeas, cilantro, onions and garlic in a food processor. Add the lemon juice and the spices.

⚜ Blend until smooth in texture. The mixture should turn into a bright green color.

⚜ Add the chickpea flour and tahini paste. Mix until well combined.

⚜ Transfer the falafel mixture into a bowl and shape to round balls. Bake the falafels for 15 minutes on each side. Remove from the oven and set on a plate.

⚜ Cover the plate with a lid and place the hose of the smoking gun under the lid.

⚜ Fill the smoking chamber with the hickory wood chips. Turn on the smoking gun and light the chips.

⚜ Infuse the falafels with the smoke for at least 3-8 minutes. Remove the lid and serve the smoked falafels with cucumber and cherry tomatoes!

SMOKED GREEN ASPARAGUS SALAD

INGREDIENTS

- 1 cup green asparagus
- ¼ cup shaved parmesan cheese
- 1 tbsp chopped pistachios
- 1 tbsp lemon juice
- 1 tsp honey
- 1 pinch sea salt and black pepper
- 3 tbsp extra virgin olive oil
- 1 garlic clove, minced

Prep Time	5 Min.
Cooking Time	10 Min.
Smoking Time	3-5 Min.
Portion	2
Category	SNACK

INSTRUCTIONS

In a small bowl combine the lemon juice, olive oil, honey and garlic.
Season with salt, pepper and set aside.

Shave the green asparagus and slice the asparagus into thin slices.

In another bowl toss the shaved parmesan with the asparagus shavings and pistachios. Drizzle the lemon dressing over the salad and combine well.

Cover the salad with film and place the lid under it.
Fill the smoking chamber with the wood chips and cover the wood.
Let the salad infuse for 3-5 minutes with the smoke.

Remove the film or lid and serve immediately!

SMOKED ASIAN CHICKEN WINGS

INGREDIENTS

- 10 chicken wings
- 1 tbsp Soy sauce
- 1 tsp sesame seeds
- 1 tbsp sesame oil
- ½ bunch of coriander
- 1 lime, cut into wedges
- pecan wood chips

Prep Time	15 Min.
Cooking Time	30 Min.
Smoking Time	5-10 Min.
Portion	2
Category	SNACK

INSTRUCTIONS

In a small bowl mix together the soy sauce, sesame seeds and sesame oil.
Marinate the chicken wings in this mixture for 10 minutes.

Preheat the oven to 390 °F.

Place the marinated chicken wings on a baking sheet and bake in the oven for 30 minutes or until the chicken is crispy.

Remove from the oven and cover the chicken wings with plastic wrap.
Place the hose under the plastic wrap.
Fill the smoking chamber with the pecan wood chips.
Turn on the smoking gun and light the chips.

Infuse the chicken wings with the smoke for at least 5-10 minutes.
Remove the lid and serve the wings crispy and hot!
Garnish with lime slices and coriander.

SMOKED BAKED BRIE

INGREDIENTS

- 1 Brie Cheese Wheel
- 1 tbsp candied almonds, chopped
- ¼ cup honey
- pinch of salt
- 1 pear, sliced
- pear wood chips

Prep Time	5 Min.	
Cooking Time	15 Min.	
Smoking Time	3-5 Min.	
Portion	4	
Category	SNACK	

INSTRUCTIONS

- Preheat the oven to 375 °F.
  In a small bowl toss together the honey, almonds and salt.

- Place the Brie on a baking sheet and top with the honey mixture.
  Bake for 10 minutes in the oven.
  Remove the Brie from the oven and sprinkle with the almonds.

- Place a lid over the baked Brie and place the hose under the lid.
  Fill the smoking chamber with the hickory wood chips.
  Turn on the smoking gun and light the chips.

- Infuse the Brie with the smoke for at least 3-5 minutes.
  Remove the lid and serve the Baked Brie with pear slices.

SMOKED CANDIED ALMONDS

INGREDIENTS

- 1 cup Almonds, raw
- 1 egg white
- 1 tsp vanilla extract
- pinch of sea salt
- ¼ cup granulated sugar
- 1 tsp ground cinnamon
- pecan wood chips

Prep Time	5 Min.
Cooking Time	15 Min.
Smoking Time	3-5 Min.
Portion	4
Category	SNACK

INSTRUCTIONS

In a small bowl combine sugar, sea salt and cinnamon and set aside.

In a large bowl, whip egg white and vanilla extract with a whisk until frothy.

Add the almonds to the wet mixture and stir until well coated. Now add the dry ingredients to the almonds and spread them evenly on a baking sheet.

Bake at 360 °F for 15 minutes or until caramelized.
Remove the almonds from the oven and place in a bowl.
Cover the bowl with a lid and place the hose of the smoking gun under it.
Light the wood chips in the smoking chamber and fill the bowl with smoke.

Infuse the Almonds with the smoke for at least 3-5 minutes.
Serve the Almonds immediately!

SMOKED CHICKEN WRAP BITES

INGREDIENTS

- 2 chicken breasts
- 1 tsp smoked paprika
- ½ tsp garlic powder
- pinch of salt
- 4 tortillas
- 5 oz. mozzarella cheese
- 4 large iceberg
- 2 tbsp mayonnaise
- 1 tsp chipotle chili powder
- apple wood chips

Prep Time	10 Min.
Cooking Time	10 Min.
Smoking Time	5-10 Min.
Portion	4
Category	SNACK

INSTRUCTIONS

- Season the chicken breasts with salt, smoked paprika and garlic powder. In a small bowl combine the mayonnaise and the chipotle chili powder. Set aside.

- Heat oil in a pan and cook the chicken breast on both sides until the chicken is cooked throughly. Remove the chicken from the pan and let it rest on a cutting board for 5 minutes.

- Cut the chicken breast in bite sized pieces. Place a lid over the chicken breast and place the hose under the lid. Fill the smoking chamber with the apple wood chips. Turn on the smoking gun and light the chips.

- Infuse the chicken breast pieces with the smoke for at least 5-10 minutes.

- To assemble the chicken wraps, layer the lettuce leaves, add the chicken, mozzarella cheese and a drizzle of the chipotle mayonnaise. Close the wraps and place on a grill pan. Cook for 2 minutes on both sides until the cheese is melted.

- Remove from the grill pan and slice the wraps onto bite sized pieces. Serve!

SMOKED CORN ON THE COB

INGREDIENTS

- 3 corn on the cob
- ¼ cup butter
- pinch of sea salt
- pinch of black pepper
- ¼ tsp cayenne pepper
- hickory wood chips

Prep Time	5 Min.
Cooking Time	20 Min.
Smoking Time	5-15 Min.
Portion	4
Category	SNACK

INSTRUCTIONS

🌿 Clean the corn but dont remove the husks.
Soak the corn in cold water for at least 1 hour.

🌿 Remove the corn from the water and pull back the husks. Set aside.

🌿 Combine the butter, black pepper, cayenne pepper and salt in a small bowl.
Brush the butter mixture over the corn cob.
Bake the corn in the oven for 20 minutes at 180 degrees until soft.

🌿 Place the corn on a plate and cover with the glass bowl.
Smoke the corn for 15 minutes.

🌿 Serve the smoked corn cob with some extra butter!

SMOKED GARLIC BUTTER

INGREDIENTS

- 1 cup butter, unsalted and softened
- ½ clove garlic, chopped
- herbs of your choice
- pinch of sea salt
- oak wood chips

Prep Time	5 Min.
Smoking Time	5-10 Min.
Portion	2
Category	SNACK

INSTRUCTIONS

☀ Cut the soft butter into cubes and combine with the chopped garlic and herbs.

☀ Combine well then place in a zip lock bag.

☀ Place the hose from the smoking gun into the top of the bag, then close the bag tightly. Light the wood chips and fill the bag with smoke. Remove the hose and close the bag.

☀ Let the smoke infuse for at least 5-10 minutes.

☀ Remove the butter from the bag and transfer to a bowl.
Whip the butter using a hand mixer.

☀ Transfer the smoked butter to a bowl and store in the fridge.

SMOKED MOZZARELLA STICKS

INGREDIENTS

- 6 mozzarella sticks
- 1 egg
- 1 tbsp milk
- ½ cup flour
- 1 cup bread crumbs
- ½ tsp italian seasoning
- ¼ tsp garlic powder
- apple wood chips

Prep Time	10 Min.
Cooking Time	5 Min.
Smoking Time	3-5 Min.
Portion	2
Category	SNACK

INSTRUCTIONS

- Preheat the deep fryer to 300 °F.

- In a small bowl combine bread crumbs, Italian seasoning and garlic powder. Mix well and set aside.

- In another bowl mix together milk and eggs.

- Dredge the mozzarella sticks in flour, dip in the milk mixture then roll in the bread-crumbs mix.

  Deep fry the mozzarella sticks for 2 minutes until crispy and golden brown.

- Remove from the deep fryer and drain on a paper towel.

  Place the hose under the plastic wrap.

  Fill the smoking chamber with the apple wood chips.

  Turn on the smoking gun and light the chips.

- Infuse the zucchini fries with the smoke for at least 3-5 minutes.

  Remove the lid and serve the zucchini fries crispy and hot!

SMOKED PIZZA TOAST BITES

INGREDIENTS

- 2 slices of bread, toast
- ¼ cup pizza sauce or tomato sauce
- ½ tsp dried oregano
- ½ cup mozzarella, grated
- topping of your choice
- cherry wood chips

Prep Time	10 Min.
Cooking Time	5 Min.
Smoking Time	3-5 Min.
Portion	2
Category	SNACK

INSTRUCTIONS

🌿 Preheat the oven to 375 °F.

🌿 Place the toast on a baking sheet and spread with the pizza sauce.
Top the toast with some mozzarella cheese and the topping of your choice.
Sprinkle dried Oregano over the toast.
Place in the oven and let the cheese melt.
Remove from the oven and transfer to a plate.

🌿 Cover the toast with plastic wrap.
Place the hose under the plastic wrap.
Fill the smoking chamber with the cherry wood chips.
Turn on the smoking gun and light the chips.

🌿 Infuse the toast with the smoke for at least 3-5 minutes.
Remove the lid and serve the smoked pizza toast bites!

SMOKED ROSEMARY POPCORN

INGREDIENTS

- 1 popcorn bag
- ½ tsp dried rosemary
- ½ tsp paprika powder
- pinch of sea salt
- 1 tbsp butter, melted
- hickory wood chips

Prep Time	5 Min.
Smoking Time	3-5 Min.
Portion	2
Category	SNACK

INSTRUCTIONS

☆ Place the popcorn in a bowl and combine with the paprika powder and dried rosemary. Drizzle the melted butter over the popcorn, then stir well until combined.

☆ Place a lid or plastic wrap and the hose on the bowl and cover tightly. Fill the smoking chamber with the hickory wood chips. Turn on the smoking gun and light the chips.

☆ Fill the bowl with smoke and remove the hose, keeping the lid on.

☆ Infuse the popcorn with the smoke for at least 3-5 minutes.

☆ Remove the lid and enjoy the smoky popcorn!

SMOKED SALMON CRACKERS

INGREDIENTS

- 12 crackers of your favorite brand
- ½ cup cream cheese, softened
- 4 oz smoked salmon
- ½ large cucumber, sliced
- 1 sprig of dill
- pinch of sea salt
- pinch of black pepper
- pear wood chips

Prep Time	5 Min.
Smoking Time	3-5 Min.
Portion	12 crackers
Category	SNACK

INSTRUCTIONS

Spread the cream cheese evenly on the crackers.
Season with salt and pepper.

Slice the cucumber into ½ inch thick slices and place one slice on each cracker.
Place a piece of smoked salmon on top and garnish with dill leaves.

Place a lid over the crackers and place the hose under the lid.
Fill the smoking chamber with the pear wood chips.
Turn on the smoking gun and light the chips.

Infuse the crackers with the smoke for at least 3-5 minutes.
Remove the lid and serve the crackers!

SMOKED SPINACH AND BROCCOLI SOUP

INGREDIENTS

- 1 ½ cup Broccoli florets
- 1 cup Spinach, chopped
- 2 cloves garlic, minced
- 1 onion, finely chopped
- ½ cup coconut milk
- 1 tbsp butter
- 1 cup vegetable stock
- bread croutons for garnish
- cotton wood chips

Prep Time	10 Min.
Cooking Time	15 Min.
Smoking Time	3-5 Min.
Portion	2
Category	SNACK

INSTRUCTIONS

Heat a pan on low heat and add the butter.
Saute the garlic and onions for 5 minutes in the butter until they turn translucent.

Add the broccoli and stir well. Add the vegetable stock and cook until the broccoli is soft.

Add the Spinach, coconut milk and taste with salt and pepper. Puree the soup with a hand blender.

Place the lid over the soup pot and fill the smoking chamber with the cotton wood chips. Turn on the smoking gun and light the chips.

Fill the bowl with smoke and remove the hose, keeping the lid on.

Infuse the soup with the smoke for at least 3-5 minutes.

Remove the bowl and serve the soup hot!

SMOKED TOMATO SOUP

INGREDIENTS

• 1 lb tomatoes, chopped	**Prep Time** 5 Min.
• 2 cloves garlic, chopped	**Cooking Time** 30 Min.
• 1 onion, diced	**Smoking Time** 5 Min.
• 1 tbsp extra virgin olive oil	**Portion** 4
• pinch of sea salt	**Category** SNACK
• pinch of black pepper	
• 1 sprig fresh basil leaves	
• ½ cup vegetable stock	
• ¼ cup heavy cream	
• ¼ cup croutons	
• cotton wood chips	

INSTRUCTIONS

🌿 In a large pot add the olive oil and heat on medium high heat.

Add the onions, garlic and tomatoes to the pot.

Season with salt and pepper.

🌿 Roast the tomatoes for 5 minutes then add the vegetable stock.

Boil the soup for 25 minutes, then add the basil leaves.

🌿 Transfer the soup to a blender and mix until smooth in texture.

Add the cream and bring to a boil.

🌿 Transfer the tomato soup to bowls then cover with a lid and place the hose of the smoking gun under it. Fill the smoking chamber with the cotton wood chips.

Turn on the smoking gun and light the chips.

Fill the bowl with smoke and remove the hose, keeping the lid on.

Infuse the tomato soup with the smoke for at least 5 minutes.

🌿 Remove the lid.

🌿 Serve the tomato soup with croutons and garnish with fresh basil leaves.

SMOKED BAGEL & SALMON

INGREDIENTS

- 2 bagels
- smoked salmon
- 1 cucumber, sliced
- 1 tbsp pickled red onions
- pinch of black pepper
- fresh dill leaves
- 2 tbsp creme fraiche
- hickory wood chips

Prep Time	5 Min.
Smoking Time	5 Min.
Portion	2
Category	SNACK

INSTRUCTIONS

🌿 In a small bowl combine the dill leaves and the creme fraiche.

Season with the fresh black pepper.

Combine well then set aside.

🌿 Toast the bagels and cut in half.

Spread the creme fraiche on each side and top with the cucumbers and smoked salmon.

🌿 Cover the bagels with a lid and place the hose of the smoking gun under it.

Fill the smoking chamber with the hickory wood chips.

Turn on the smoking gun and light the chips.

Fill the bowl with smoke and remove the hose, keeping the lid on.

Infuse the bagels with the smoke for at least 5 minutes.

🌿 Remove the lid.

🌿 Serve the smoked salmon bagels with pickled red onions on the side. Enjoy!

SMOKED GREEK SALAD

INGREDIENTS

- 4 roma tomatoes
- 2 small cucumber
- ½ cup feta cheese
- sprig of mint leaves
- 2 tbsp extra virgin olive oil
- 1 tbsp lemon juice
- pinch of salt and black pepper
- ¼ cup croutons
- 1 tsp rosemary, chopped
- pear wood chips

Prep Time	10 Min.
Smoking Time	5 Min.
Portion	2
Category	SNACK

INSTRUCTIONS

- To make the dressing combine olive oil and lemon juice in a bowl.
  Mix well until combined then season with salt and pepper. set aside.

- In a separate bowl combine all the other ingredients then mix with the dressing.
  Toss well until combined.

- Cover the greek salad with a lid and place the hose of the smoking gun under it.
  Fill the smoking chamber with the pear wood chips.
  Turn on the smoking gun and light the chips.
  Fill the bowl with smoke and remove the hose, keeping the lid on.
  Infuse the greek salad with the smoke for at least 4 minutes.

- Remove the lid.

- Serve the smoked greek salad cold and garnish with mint leaves. Enjoy!

SMOKED AVOCADO SALAD

INGREDIENTS

- 2 tomatoes, diced
- 2 cucumbers, diced
- ½ small red onion
- 1 avocado, cored and diced
- 1 tbsp olive oil
- 1 tsp red wine vinegar
- ½ tsp dried oregano
- pinch of sea salt
- pinch of black pepper
- cherry wood chips

Prep Time	5 Min.
Smoking Time	5-10 Min.
Portion	2
Category	SNACK

INSTRUCTIONS

Cut the tomatoes and cucumbers in bite size pieces.
Cut the avocado in half and remove the core.
Next remove the skin and cut the avocado in small pieces.

Place the cucumbers, tomatoes, avocado and red onions in a bowl.

In a small bowl, whisk together the red wine vinegar, olive oil, oregano, sea salt and pepper. Mix well. Pour the dressing over the salad and toss well.

Cover the avocado salad with a lid and place the hose of the smoking gun under it. Fill the smoking chamber with the cherry wood chips. Turn on the smoking gun and light the chips. Fill the bowl with smoke and remove the hose, keeping the lid on. Infuse the avocado salad with the smoke for at least 5-10 minutes.

Remove the lid.

Serve the smoked avocado salad cold!

SMOKED ASIAN PORK BALLS

INGREDIENTS

- 2 cups basmati rice
- 1 lb ground pork
- ¼ cup bread crumbs
- 1 large egg
- 1 tbsp garlic, chopped
- ½ tbsp ginger, grated
- 2 kaffir lime leaves, chopped
- 1 stalk lemongrass, chopped
- pinch of black pepper and salt
- hickory wood chips

Prep Time	10 Min.
Cooking Time	30 Min.
Smoking Time	5 Min.
Portion	4
Category	SNACK

INSTRUCTIONS

- Rinse and drain the rice in cold water. Place the rice in a pot with 1 ½ cup of water and bring to a boil. Reduce the heat and cook slowly with a lid for 15 minutes until the rice is cooked. Let the rice sit covered for 10 minutes then set aside.

- In a bowl combine the pork, breadcrumbs, egg, garlic, ginger, kaffir lime leaves and lemongrass. Season with salt and pepper. Mix the pork mixture well then form into meatballs. Place them on a greased baking sheet and cook in the oven for 15 minutes at 360 °F.

- Remove the meatballs from the oven and set aside.

- Divide the rice between 4 bowls and top with the meatballs. Cover the bowls with a lid and place the hose of the smoking gun under it. Fill the smoking chamber with the hickory wood chips. Turn on the smoking gun and light the chips. Fill the bowl with smoke and remove the hose, keeping the lid on. Infuse the rice bowls with the smoke for at least 5 minutes. Remove the lid.

- Serve the smoked meatballs with the rice and garnish with some chopped kaffir lime leaves!

MAIN COURSE

69

SMOKED YELLOW RICE CHICKEN

INGREDIENTS

- 1 pound chicken tenders
- pinch of saffron threads
- 2 tbsp olive oil
- 1 onion, diced
- 2 garlic cloves, minced
- 1 cup basmati rice
- 1 tsp turmeric powder
- ½ tsp paprika powder
- 1 cup chicken broth
- ½ cup boiling water
- 2 cardamom pods
- 1 small cucumber, sliced
- oak wood chips

Prep Time	5 Min.
Cooking Time	25 Min.
Smoking Time	3-5 Min.
Portion	4
Category	MAIN

INSTRUCTIONS

- Season the chicken with salt and pepper from both sides.

- In a pan on medium high heat, add the olive oil and heat. Add the chicken tenders and brown on both sides. Remove and set aside.

- In the same pot add the onions and saute for 2 minutes. Now add the garlic and cook for 1 minute.

- Add rice, turmeric, paprika powder, cardamom and saffron. Pour in chicken broth and boiling water. Cover and cook for 20 minutes until the rice is cooked. Transfer the rice to a plate and top with the cooked chicken tenders.

- Cover the Rice dish with the lid and place the hose under the lid. Fill the smoking chamber with the oak wood chips. Turn on the smoking gun and light the chips. Fill the bowl with smoke and remove the hose, keeping the lid on. Infuse the Yellow Rice with the smoke for 3-5 minutes. Remove the lid.

- Serve the smoked yellow rice with some fresh cucumbers. Enjoy!

SMOKED SPINACH CHEESE GRATIN

INGREDIENTS

- 3 oz frozen Spinach
- ½ cup mozzarella cheese
- 1 tbsp butter
- 1 clove garlic, minced
- ¼ tsp nutmeg powder
- ¼ cup flour
- 2 cups milk
- ¼ cup parmesan cheese
- black pepper
- hickory wood chips

Prep Time	5 Min.
Cooking Time	20 Min.
Smoking Time	3-5 Min.
Portion	2
Category	MAIN

INSTRUCTIONS

Preheat the oven to 390 °F. Place a large pan on medium high heat and melt the butter. Add the garlic and cook for 1 minute.

Add the flour, cook and stir constantly for 1 minute. Add milk, salt and nutmeg and stir until combined. Bring to a boil then simmer for 5 minutes until thickened.

Add the Spinach and parmesan to the sauce and combine well. Season with salt and pepper.

Transfer the mixture to a baking dish and sprinkle with the mozzarella cheese. Bake for 20 minutes in the oven until the cheese is melted and turned golden. Remove from the oven and set aside.

Cover the Gratin with the lid and place the hose under the lid. Fill the smoking chamber with the apple wood chips. Turn on the smoking gun and light the chips. Fill the bowl with smoke and remove the hose, keeping the lid on. Infuse the gratin with the smoke for 3-5 minutes. Remove the lid.

Serve the smoked spinach cheese gratin with a glass of milk. Enjoy!

SMOKED SOURDOUGH SANDWICH

INGREDIENTS

- 4 slices of sourdough bread
- 2 tbsp extra virgin olive oil
- ¼ cup mayonnaise
- 6 oz cheddar cheese
- 4 oz Paris Ham
- 1 tbsp sriracha chili sauce
- ½ cup salad leaves
- hickory wood chips

Prep Time	10 Min.
Cooking Time	8 Min.
Smoking Time	3-5 Min.
Portion	2
Category	MAIN

INSTRUCTIONS

✽ Spread the mayonnaise and sriracha chili sauce on both sides of the sourdough bread. Place the paris ham on the bread and top with a slice of cheddar cheese.

Top with another slice of sourdough bread.

✽ Preheat the oven to 375 degrees F and preheat a non-stick pan on medium high heat.

✽ Add the olive oil to the pan then place the sourdough sandwich on it. Weigh down the sandwich with another pan on top.

Cook for about 3 minutes on each side until the bread turns golden brown.

✽ Top one side of the sandwich with some more cheddar cheese, then cook in the oven for 2 minutes until the cheese is melted and browned.

Remove the sandwich from the oven and transfer to a plate.

✽ Cover the Sourdough Sandwich with the lid and place the hose under the lid. Fill the smoking chamber with the apple wood chips. Turn on the smoking gun and light the chips. Fill the bowl with smoke and remove the hose, keeping the lid on. Infuse the sourdough sandwich with the smoke for 3-5 minutes.

Remove the lid.

✽ Serve the smoked Sourdough Sandwich with the fresh salad leaves and sprinkle with some olive oil.

SMOKED SALMON STEAK

INGREDIENTS

- 2 Salmon Steaks
- 1 cup frozen edamame
- 2 tbsp olive oil
- 1 tsp soy sauce
- 1 cup jasmine rice
- white sesame, toasted
- 2 garlic cloves
- 1 sprig of coriander
- pinch of sea salt
- pinch of black pepper
- hickory wood chips

Prep Time	5 Min.
Cooking Time	10 Min.
Smoking Time	5-8 Min.
Portion	2
Category	MAIN

INSTRUCTIONS

- Preheat a grill or pan on high heat.

- Season the Salmon steaks with salt, pepper and marinate with the garlic and olive oil. Once the pan is hot, place the salmon steaks skin side down in the pan. Cook for 5 minutes on the skin side then flip it and cook for another 5 minutes until the meat is cooked. Set aside.

- Add the olive oil to the same pan, then add the garlic and edamame. Cook for 2 minutes until the edamame is warmed. Add the soy sauce, then set the edamame aside.

  Transfer the Salmon Steaks on a plate. Cover the Salmon Steaks with the lid and place the hose under the lid. Fill the smoking chamber with the apple wood chips. Turn on the smoking gun and light the chips. Fill the bowl with smoke and remove the hose, keeping the lid on. Infuse the salmon steaks with the smoke for 5-8 minutes.

  Remove the lid.

- Serve the smoked salmon steaks with the cooked edamame and sprinkle with the toasted sesame seeds.

SMOKED PORK CHOP & FRIES

INGREDIENTS

- 2 large pork chops
- 1 cup sweet potato fries
- 2 tbsp olive oil
- pinch of sea salt
- black pepper
- 1 sprig fresh rosemary
- 1 tbsp mustard
- 2 garlic cloves, minced
- apple wood chips

Prep Time	10 Min.
Cooking Time	15 Min.
Smoking Time	5-10 Min.
Portion	2
Category	MAIN

INSTRUCTIONS

- Preheat a grill or pan on high heat.

- Marinate the pork chops with olive oil, mustard, garlic, salt and pepper.

- Add some olive oil to the hot pan and sear the pork chops for 5 minutes on each side until the meat is cooked throughly.

- Meanwhile, fry the sweet potato fries for 3 minutes until crispy and golden brown.

  Set aside.

  Transfer the Pork chops on a plate. Cover the pork chops with the lid and place the hose under the lid. Fill the smoking chamber with the apple wood chips. Turn on the smoking gun and light the chips. Fill the bowl with smoke and remove the hose, keeping the lid on. Infuse the pork chops with the smoke for 5-10 minutes.

  Remove the lid.

- Serve the smoked pork chops with the sweet potato fries and some more mustard on the side.

SMOKED ITALIAN PINSA

INGREDIENTS

Pinsa dough:

- 3 cups flour
- ½ cup rice flour
- 1 cup water, cold
- 1 tbsp extra virgin olive oi
- ½ tsp dry yeast
- 1 tsp salt

Topping:

- 1 cup pizza sauce
- 12 slices salami
- 10 oz mozzarella cheese
- rocket leaves
- 2 dry red chilies

Prep Time	20 Min.
Cooking Time	10 Min.
Smoking Time	3-5 Min.
Portion	2 pinsa
Category	MAIN

INSTRUCTIONS

- Preheat the oven to 430 °F.

- In a large bowl combine the flour, rice flour and yeast. While whisking, add cold water. Now add the olive oil and salt. Mix well until combined.

- Cover the bowl with a plastic wrap and leave to rise to room temperature for 1 hour. Place the dough in the fridge for 24 hours or overnight.

- Divide the dough into two parts and form a round ball. Cover the dough with a towel and let rise for 60 minutes.

- Stretch the dough in an oval pinsa shape. Top the pinsa dough with the pizza sauce, salami slices and mozzarella cheese.

- Bake the pinsa for 10 minutes in the oven until the dough is crispy.

- Place the pinsa on a plate and cover with the lid. Place the hose under the lid. Fill the smoking chamber with the cherry wood chips. Turn on the smoking gun and light the chips. Fill the bowl with smoke and remove the hose, keeping the lid on. Infuse the Pinsa with the smoke for 3-5 minutes. Remove the lid.

- Garnish with some rocket leaves and dry chilies.

SMOKED BEEF HAMBURGER

INGREDIENTS

- 1 pound ground beef
- 1 egg
- 1 tsp dijon mustard
- 1 cup onion, chopped
- 1 tsp worcestershire sauce
- pinch of salt and pepper
- 1/2 cup green salad leaves
- 1 tomato, sliced
- ½ onion, sliced
- 4 burger buns
- pecan wood chips

Prep Time	5 Min.
Cooking Time	10 Min.
Smoking Time	3-5 Min.
Portion	2
Category	MAIN

INSTRUCTIONS

⚜ Preheat a grill or pan on high heat.

⚜ Melt butter in the pan and saute until soft and golden. Set aside.

⚜ In a large bowl combine the ground beef, cooked onions, egg, mustard and worcestershire sauce. Mix by hand until well combined. Season with salt and pepper.

⚜ Portion the mixture into patties and sear the patties in the pan for 5 minutes on each side. Transfer the burgers on a plate.

⚜ Cover the burger patties with the lid and place the hose under the lid. Fill the smoking chamber with the pecan wood chips. Turn on the smoking gun and light the chips. Fill the bowl with smoke and remove the hose, keeping the lid on. Infuse the burger patties with the smoke for 3-5 minutes. Remove the lid.

⚜ Transfer the burger patties on the burger buns and top with salad leaves, tomato and onion slices. Serve with a sauce of your Choice.

SMOKED GRILLED SAUSAGES

INGREDIENTS

- 1 lb spicy italian sausages
- 1 cup mixed green salad leaves
- 2 tbsp fresh lemon juice
- 2 tbsp extra virgin olive oil
- 1 tbsp green olives, sliced
- pinch of sea salt
- pinch of fresh black pepper
- 1 tbsp yellow mustard
- pecan wood chips

Prep Time	5 Min.
Cooking Time	20 Min.
Smoking Time	5-10 Min.
Portion	2
Category	MAIN

INSTRUCTIONS

Prepare a grill or a pan for medium high heat.

In a bowl combine the green salad leaves with the sliced green olives. Drizzle with the oil, lemon juice and season with salt and pepper.

Grill Sausages until brown, about 5 minutes per side.

Transfer the sausages to an oven and cook for 10 minutes at 375 °F, until cooked through.

Transfer the sausage to a plate. Cover with the lid and place the hose under the lid. Fill the smoking chamber with the pecan wood chips. Turn on the smoking gun and light the chips. Fill the bowl with smoke and remove the hose, keeping the lid on.

Infuse the Sausages with the smoke for 5-10 minutes.

Remove the lid.

Serve the grilled Sausages with the salad and yellow mustard.

SMOKED CHICKEN TERIYAKI

INGREDIENTS

- 1 lb Chicken Breast
- 2 tbsp Teriyaki Sauce
- ½ tsp white sesame, toasted
- 4 Pak Choi
- 2 garlic cloves, sliced
- 1 tbsp Sesame oil
- pinch of black pepper
- pecan wood chips

Prep Time	10 Min.
Cooking Time	10 Min.
Smoking Time	3-7 Min.
Portion	2
Category	MAIN

INSTRUCTIONS

- Prepare a pan for medium high heat.

- Marinate the chicken breast with the teriyaki sauce and black pepper. Allow to marinate for 10 minutes.

- Sear the Chicken breast from both sides for 5 minutes, until the chicken breast is cooked throughly. Transfer the chicken breast to a cutting board and slice. In the same pan add the sesame oil, garlic and pak choi. Cook until the pak choi is cooked.

- Transfer the chicken breast and pak choi to a plate. Cover with the lid and place the hose under the lid.

- Fill the smoking chamber with the pecan wood chips, turn on the smoking gun and light the chips. Fill the bowl with smoke and remove the hose, keeping the lid on. Infuse the chicken breast with the smoke for 3-7 minutes.

- Remove the lid.

- Serve the Chicken Teriyaki sliced with the pak choi and sprinkle with toasted sesame seeds.

SMOKED BEEF STEAK & BROCCOLI

INGREDIENTS

- ½ lb sirloin Steak
- 1 Broccoli head, florets
- 1 tbsp extra virgin olive oil
- 1 tbsp butter
- 2 Garlic cloves, minced
- rosemary, chopped
- ½ Lemon
- pinch of black pepper
- pinch of sea salt
- Cherry wood chips

Prep Time	10 Min.
Cooking Time	10 Min.
Smoking Time	3-5 Min.
Portion	2
Category	MAIN

INSTRUCTIONS

- Prepare a grill or a pan on medium high heat.

- Marinate the sirloin steak with olive oil, chopped rosemary, salt and pepper. Allow to marinate for 30 minutes.

- Break down the broccoli head into pieces. Cook them in boiling water for 2 minutes, then rinse with the cold water. Heat butter in a large pan then add the sirloin steak. Sear the steak for 2 minutes on each side until browned. Set aside.

- In the same pan add the garlic, lemon juice and broccoli florets. Cook until the broccoli is brown.

- Transfer the sirloin steak to a plate. Cover with the lid and place the hose under the lid. Fill the smoking chamber with the cherry wood chips. Turn on the smoking gun and light the chips. Fill the bowl with smoke and remove the hose, keeping the lid on. Infuse the Steak with the smoke for 3-5 minutes.

- Remove the lid.

- Serve the Sirloin steak sliced with the broccoli and lemon slices!

SMOKED PRAWN WONTONS

INGREDIENTS

- 12 wonton wrappers
- ½ lb raw prawns
- 1 cm piece of ginger
- 1 clove garlic, minced
- 1 tsp dry sherry wine
- 1 tbsp soy sauce
- ¼ tsp sesame oil
- ½ tsp sichuan pepper
- white sesame seeds, toasted
- apple wood chips

Prep Time	10 Min.
Cooking Time	2 Min.
Smoking Time	5-10 Min.
Portion	4
Category	MAIN

INSTRUCTIONS

Peel and dice the prawn meat and keep in a bowl. Slice the ginger in thin stripes and add to the prawn meat together with the minced garlic, soy sauce, sesame oil, sichuan pepper and sherry wine. Combine well.

Cover the bowl and refrigerate for 15 minutes.

For each wonton, place one teaspoon of the prawn mixture in the center of each wrapper. Moisten one edge of the wrapper with some water, then fold it in half and close the wonton. In a large pot bring water to a boil and add the wontons.

Cook for 2 minutes then set aside.

Cover the cooked prawn wontons with the lid and place the hose under the lid. Fill the smoking chamber with the apple wood chips. Turn on the smoking gun and light the chips. Fill the bowl with smoke and remove the hose, keeping the lid on. Infuse the prawn wontons with the smoke for 5-10 minutes. Remove the lid.

Serve the smoked prawn wontons with some extra soy sauce and sprinkle with the toasted sesame seeds.

SMOKED PRAWN CAESAR SALAD

INGREDIENTS

- 1 lb shrimps
- 1 tbsp extra virgin olive oil
- 1 big romaine lettuce, torn
- ½ cup parmesan cheese, grated
- ¼ cup croutons

For the dressing:
- ½ cup mayonnaise
- 1 tbsp lemon juice
- 2 tsp dijon mustard
- 2 tsp Worcestershire sauce
- 1 tsp anchovies
- 1 clove garlic, minced
- pinch of black pepper
- hickory wood chips

Prep Time	10 Min.
Cooking Time	6 Min.
Smoking Time	3-7 Min.
Portion	4
Category	MAIN

INSTRUCTIONS

- To make the dressing combine the mayonnaise with the lemon juice mustard, worcestershire sauce, anchovies, garlic and black pepper. Cover and refrigerate.

- Heat olive oil in a frying pan on medium high heat, then add the shrimps and cook for 3 minutes on each side. Remove from the heat.

- Cover the shrimps with the lid and place the hose under the lid. Fill the smoking chamber with the hickory wood chips. Turn on the smoking gun and light the chips. Fill the bowl with smoke and remove the hose, keeping the lid on. Infuse the shrimps with the smoke for 3-7 minutes. Remove the lid.

- In a large bowl place the lettuce and coat with the dressing. Add the smoked shrimps, croutons and parmesan cheese.

- Serve!

SMOKED GNOCCHI & BUTTER SAGE

INGREDIENTS

- 1/2 lb potato gnocchi
- ¼ tsp nutmeg
- 1 clove garlic, smashed
- pinch of sea salt
- 2 tbsp parmesan cheese, grated
- 4 tbsp butter
- fresh sage leaves
- hickory wood chips

Prep Time	15 Min.
Cooking Time	2 Min.
Smoking Time	5-10 Min.
Portion	2
Category	MAIN

INSTRUCTIONS

Bring a large pot of salted water to a boil and add the potato gnocchis. Cook for 5 minutes or until they float to the top.

Meanwhile, melt the butter in a sauce pan and add the sage leaves and the garlic. Season with salt, pepper and nutmeg. Cook the butter for about 5 minutes until it starts to brown.

Now add the drained potato gnocchis and coat with the sage butter sauce.

Add the grated parmesan and remove from the stove.

Cover the potato gnocchis with the lid and place the hose under the lid. Fill the smoking chamber with the hickory wood chips. Turn on the smoking gun and light the chips. Fill the bowl with smoke and remove the hose, keeping the lid on. Infuse the potato gnocchis with the smoke for 5-10 minutes.

Remove the lid.

Serve potato gnocchis with grated parmesan and fried sage leaves on top!

SMOKED PARMESAN CHICKEN

INGREDIENTS

- 1 large chicken breast, cut in half lengthwise
- ¼ tsp garlic powder
- sea salt and black pepper
- 1 egg, beaten
- ½ cup breadcrumbs
- ¼ cup parmesan, grated
- ⅛ cup flour
- ¼ tsp italian seasoning
- 1 tbsp olive oil
- 1 tbsp pickled cucumbers
- pecan wood chips
- 1 lemon, wedges

Prep Time	10 Min.
Cooking Time	20 Min.
Smoking Time	3-5 Min.
Portion	2
Category	MAIN

INSTRUCTIONS

Preheat the oven to 390 °F. Pat the chicken dry with a paper towel, then sprinkle it with the garlic powder and season with salt and pepper. Prepare 3 bowls: one with the flour, one with the eggs (whisk them with a fork), and the third with the panko/parmesan/Italian seasoning. In a frying pan, heat the olive oil on medium high heat. Meanwhile, coat the chicken pieces in the flour, dip each piece in the egg, then place in the breadcrumb mixture.

Add the breaded chicken pieces to the frying pan and cook for around 2-3 minutes until golden. Transfer the pan to the oven and cook for 5 minutes or until cooked throughly.

Cover the breaded parmesan chicken with the lid and place the hose under the lid. Fill the smoking chamber with the apple wood chips. Turn on the smoking gun and light the chips. Fill the bowl with smoke and remove the hose, keeping the lid on. Infuse the breaded parmesan with the smoke for 3-5 minutes. Remove the lid.

Serve with lemon wedges and pickled cucumbers on the side!

SMOKED MEATBALL PARMESAN

INGREDIENTS

- ½ lb ground beef
- ½ lb ground pork
- ¼ cup breadcrumbs
- ⅛ cup whole milk
- 1 egg, beaten
- 2 tbsp parmesan cheese
- ½ cup mozzarella cheese
- ½ tsp italian seasoning
- ¼ tsp onion powder
- 2 tbsp extra virgin olive oil
- 1 jar pasta sauce
- pinch of sea salt and black pepper

Prep Time	20 Min.
Cooking Time	15 Min.
Smoking Time	5-10 Min.
Portion	4
Category	MAIN

INSTRUCTIONS

- Soak the breadcrumbs in the milk for 5 minutes. Press out the milk from the breadcrumbs and set aside.

- In a large bowl combine the ground beef and pork, add the whisked egg, parmesan, and soaked bread crumbs. Season with salt, pepper, Italian seasoning and onion powder.

- Form small round balls from the meat mixture and set aside. Heat a large frying pan on medium high heat and add the olive oil.

- Now add the meatballs to the pan and fry for 5 minutes until golden brown. Add the pasta sauce and cook for 10 minutes until the meatballs are cooked throughly.

- Cover the meatballs with the lid and place the hose under the lid. Fill the smoking chamber with the apple wood chips. Turn on the smoking gun and light the chips. Fill the bowl with smoke and remove the hose, keeping the lid on. Infuse the meatballs with the smoke for 5-10 minutes. Remove the lid.

- Serve the smoked prawn wontons with some extra soy sauce and sprinkle with the toasted sesame seeds.

SMOKED MEATBALL PASTA

INGREDIENTS

- 1 lb meatballs
- 14 oz linguine pasta
- 4 tbsp extra virgin olive oil
- 1 sprig of fresh italian basil, chopped
- ½ cup grated parmesan
- 1 tsp italian seasoning
- 2 garlic cloves, minced
- pinch of sea salt
- 28 oz canned crushed tomatoes
- pinch of black pepper
- 1 onion, chopped
- apple wood chips

Prep Time	10 Min.
Cooking Time	15 Min.
Smoking Time	3-5 Min.
Portion	4
Category	MAIN

INSTRUCTIONS

Bring a large pot with salted water to boil. Add the Linguine pasta and cook for 10 minutes. Drain and set aside.

In a large frying pan, heat the olive oil, then add the onions and garlic. Cook them for 5 minutes until soft.

Add the meatballs and the canned tomatoes. Boil the sauce for about 5 minutes then add the cooked Linguine pasta.

Toss and Coat the pasta with the meatball sauce. Add the chopped italian basil then transfer to a bowl or plate.

Cover the meatball pasta with the lid and place the hose under the lid. Fill the smoking chamber with the apple wood chips. Turn on the smoking gun and light the chips. Fill the bowl with smoke and remove the hose, keeping the lid on. Infuse the meatball pasta with the smoke for 3-5 minutes. Remove the lid.

Serve the smoked meatball pasta with some extra basil leaves and grated parmesan on top.

SMOKED GRILLED PRAWNS & AIOLI

INGREDIENTS

- 2 lbs tiger prawns, peeled
- 2 cloves garlic, crushed
- pinch of fresh black pepper
- pinch of sea salt
- 1 tbsp lemon juice
- 2 tbsp olive oil
- 1 sprig fresh parsley chopped

For the Aioli

- 1 cup mayonnaise
- 1 tsp lemon zest
- 2 garlic cloves, chopped
- pinch of fresh black pepper
- oak wood chips
- lime wedges for garnish

Prep Time	10 Min.
Cooking Time	10 Min.
Smoking Time	10-15 Min.
Portion	4
Category	MAIN

INSTRUCTIONS

🌿 For the Aioli combine the mayonnaise, lemon zest, garlic and fresh black pepper. Whisk until well combined then set aside.

🌿 Marinate the prawns with 1 tbsp of olive oil, lemon juice, garlic, pepper and salt.

🌿 Heat a grill or fry on high heat and add 1 tbsp of olive oil. Grill the prawns 5 minutes from both sides until cooked, then set aside

🌿 Cover the grilled Prawns with the lid and place the hose under the lid. Fill the smoking chamber with the oak wood chips. Turn on the smoking gun and light the chips. Fill the bowl with smoke and remove the hose, keeping the lid on. Infuse the Grilled Prawns with the smoke for 10-15 minutes.

🌿 Remove the lid.

🌿 Serve the smoked grilled prawns with the lemon aioli and lime wedges.

SMOKED FRENCH CAFE SANDWICH

INGREDIENTS

- 1 french baguette
- 4 tbsp truffle butter
- 6 ounces smoked french ham
- 6 leafs cos salad
- 1 tbsp mayonnaise
- 1 cup french fries
- oak wood chips

Prep Time	5 Min.
Cooking Time	5 Min.
Smoking Time	3 Min.
Portion	2
Category	MAIN

INSTRUCTIONS

⚜ Toast the baguette in the oven or in a pan until crunchy. Cut the bread in half.

⚜ Spread the mayonnaise and truffle butter on both sides of the baguette.

⚜ Fill the baguette with the smoked french ham and the cos salad.

⚜ Cover the french cafe sandwich with the lid and place the hose under the lid. Fill the smoking chamber with the apple wood chips. Turn on the smoking gun and light the chips. Fill the bowl with smoke and remove the hose, keeping the lid on. Infuse the sandwich with the smoke for 3 minutes.

⚜ Remove the lid.

⚜ Serve the smoked french cafe sandwich with french fries.

SMOKED CHICKEN MASALA

Prep Time: 15 Min.   **Cooking Time**: 30 Min.   **Smoking Time**: 3-5 Min.
Portion: 2   **Category**: MAIN

INGREDIENTS

For the Sauce

- 2 tbsp oil
- 1 tbsp butter
- 1 medium onion, chopped
- 1 clove garlic, minced
- ½ tbsp ginger
- ½ tsp ground coriander
- ½ tsp ground cumin
- ½ tsp garam masala
- 1 cup tomato sauce
- ½ cup heavy cream
- fresh coriander
- pecan wood chips

Marinade

- 20 oz Chicken thighs, diced
- 1 cup plain yogurt
- 1 tsp garam masala
- ½ tsp turmeric
- ½ tsp ground cumin
- 1 tsp ginger, grated
- 1 tbsp minced garlic
- ¼ tsp red chili powder
- ½ tsp salt

INSTRUCTIONS

- In a bowl combine all Ingredients for the marinade and marinate the chicken for 1 hour.

- In a large pot, heat oil on medium high heat. Add the chicken and cook for 2-3 minutes a side, until brown. Set aside.

- In the same pan, add butter and Onions, and cook until soft and translucent. Add Ginger and Garlic, Turmeric, Coriander Powder, Cumin, Garam Masala. Fry until fragrant.

- Add the Tomato Sauce and boil for 15 minutes on low heat, stirring occasionally until Tomato Sauce thickens. Add Chicken and cream and cook for an additional 10 minutes until the mixture is thick. Transfer the chicken masala to bowls.

- Cover the chicken masala with the lid and place the hose under the lid. Fill the smoking chamber with the pecan wood chips. Turn on the smoking gun and light the chips. Fill the bowl with smoke and remove the hose, keeping the lid on. Infuse the chicken masala with the smoke for 3-5 minutes. Remove the lid.

- Garnish with fresh Coriander and serve with hot Basmati Rice, and Naan Bread.

SMOKED CHEESY PORTOBELLO

INGREDIENTS

- 4 portobello mushrooms
- ½ cup mozzarella cheese
- 2 tbsp butter
- 1 tbsp fresh parsley
- 2 garlic cloves, chopped
- pinch of sea salt
- pinch of black pepper
- 2 sprigs fresh thyme
- apple wood chips

Prep Time	10 Min.
Cooking Time	25 Min.
Smoking Time	3-5 Min.
Portion	2
Category	MAIN

INSTRUCTIONS

Preheat the oven to 375 °F. Clean and prepare the portobello mushrooms, remove the stem and the brown gills.

In a small saucepan melt the butter, then add the garlic, thyme, salt and pepper.

Brush the butter mixture over the portobello mushrooms.

Top the mushrooms with the mozzarella cheese and bake for 25 minutes until the mushrooms are soft and the cheese is melted and golden. Remove from the oven and set aside.

Cover the portobello mushrooms with the lid and place the hose under the lid. Fill the smoking chamber with the apple wood chips. Turn on the smoking gun and light the chips. Fill the bowl with smoke and remove the hose, keeping the lid on. Infuse the mushrooms with the smoke for 3-5 minutes.

Remove the lid.

Serve the smoked portobello mushrooms with some more thyme leaves.

SMOKED PASTA SALAD

INGREDIENTS

- 2 oz pasta
- ½ cup grape tomatoes, halved
- 1 cucumber, diced
- 1 small red onion, sliced
- ¼ cup feta cheese, crumbled
- fresh parsley, chopped
- 4 tbsp extra virgin olive oil
- 2 tbsp red wine vinegar
- 1 tbsp honey
- 1 tsp dijon mustard
- pinch of salt
- pinch of black pepper
- cotton wood chips

Prep Time	10 Min.
Cooking Time	10 Min.
Smoking Time	3-5 Min.
Portion	2
Category	MAIN

INSTRUCTIONS

Bring a large pot of salted water to a boil and cook the pasta for 10 minutes until soft. Drain and rinse with cold water.

In a small bowl, combine the olive oil, vinegar, honey and mustard. Mix well until combined and season with salt and pepper.

In a large bowl combine the vegetables with the cooked pasta. Pour the dressing over the pasta and toss well. Transfer to a big serving bowl.

Cover the bowl with a lid and place the hose of the smoking gun under it.

Fill the smoking chamber with the cotton wood ships.

Turn on the smoking gun and light the chips.

Fill the bowl with smoke and remove the hose, keeping the lid on.

Infuse the pasta salad with the smoke for at least 3-5 minutes.

Remove the lid.

Serve the smoked greek pasta salad with the crumbled feta cheese. Enjoy!

SMOKED RISOTTO SAUSAGE

INGREDIENTS

- 2 Italian Pork Sausages
- 10 oz Carnaroli rice
- 1 tbsp olive oil
- ½ half Onion, chopped
- ½ cup red wine
- 2 tbsp Butter, cold
- 1 oz Parmesan, grated
- 5 cups vegetable stock
- ½ tbsp fresh rosemary, chopped
- 1 sprig Parsley leaves
- apple Wood Chips

Prep Time	10 Min.
Cooking Time	20 Min.
Smoking Time	3-5 Min.
Portion	2
Category	MAIN

INSTRUCTIONS

- In a large pan, heat the olive oil on medium high heat and saute the onions until soft for 2 minutes.

- Remove the Sausages from the cases and roll them into small balls. Fry the sausage balls in the same pan until golden brown.

- Add the Carnaroli Rice and fry for 2 minutes. Pour the stock one cup at a time, stirring all the time. The rice should be done after 20 minutes of cooking.

- Remove the pan from the heat and stir in the rosemary, parmesan and butter. Transfer the Risotto onto plates and garnish with the sausage balls and parsley.

- Cover the plates with a lid and place the hose of the smoking gun under it. Fill the smoking chamber with the apple wood chips. Turn on the smoking gun and light the chips. Fill the bowl with smoke and remove the hose, keeping the lid on. Infuse the Risotto with the smoke for at least 3-5 minutes.

- Remove the lid.

- Serve the smoked risotto sausage immediately and garnish with some more shaved parmesan.

SMOKED LAMB PITAS

Prep Time: 10 Min. **Cooking Time**: 8 Min. **Smoking Time**: 7 Min.
Portion: 4 **Category**: MAIN

INGREDIENTS

- 1 lb lamb minced
- 1 onion, chopped
- ½ cup breadcrumbs
- 1 egg
- 2 garlic cloves, chopped
- 1 sprig cilantro leaves, chopped
- ¼ tsp cumin
- ½ tsp paprika
- ½ tsp salt
- 1 tbsp olive oil

Yogurt sauce

- 1 cup yogurt
- 1 lemon, juiced
- 1 cloves garlic, chopped
- 1 tbsp fresh mint, chopped
- pinch of salt and pepper
- 4 flatbreads
- lemon wedges

INSTRUCTIONS

In a small bowl combine the yogurt, garlic, mint lemon juice and season with salt and pepper. Set aside.

Mix the minced lamb, onions, garlic, breadcrumbs, cilantro and the spices in a bowl. Mix well until combined.

Roll the mixture into balls and thread it on a small skewer and make an oval shape. Heat oil in a large pan and cook the skewers 4 minutes from each side until cooked.

Transfer the skewers on a plate and cover with a lid and place the hose of the smoking gun under it.

Fill the smoking chamber with the oak wood chips.

Turn on the smoking gun and light the chips.

Fill the bowl with smoke and remove the hose, keeping the lid on.

Infuse the lamb skewers with the smoke for at least 7 minutes.

Remove the lid.

Serve the smoked lamb skewers on the flatbreads and garnish with lemon wedges and yogurt sauce. Enjoy!

SMOKED CHICKEN SATAY

INGREDIENTS

- 2 chicken thighs, bite size pieces
- 1 stalk lemongrass, chopped
- 1 shallot, chopped
- 1 tsp ginger, minced
- ½ tbsp ground coriander
- ½ tsp cumin
- ½ tbsp soy sauce
- 1 tbsp fish sauce
- 1 tbsp brown sugar
- 1 tbsp vegetable oil
- pinch of sea salt
- wooden skewers
- cherry wood chips

Prep Time	20 Min.
Cooking Time	10 Min.
Smoking Time	5 Min.
Portion	2
Category	MAIN

INSTRUCTIONS

- Marinate the chicken thigh pieces with the lemongrass, shallots, ginger, coriander, cumin, soy sauce, fish sauce and vegetable oil. Let marinate in the fridge for at least 30 minutes.

- Soak the wooden skewers in water to prevent them from burning later while cooking.

- Preheat a pan or grill to high heat. Place the chicken pieces on the skewers and season with salt. Heat a small amount of oil in the pan, then sear the skewers on medium high heat for 10 minutes.

- Move the skewers to a plate, cover with a lid and place the hose of the smoking gun under it. Fill the smoking chamber with the cherry wood chips. Turn on the smoking gun and light the chips. Fill the bowl with smoke and remove the hose, keeping the lid on. Infuse the chicken satay with the smoke for at least 5 minutes. Remove the lid.

- Serve the smoked chicken skewers with a thai peanut sauce. Enjoy!

SMOKED BEEF CURRY

INGREDIENTS

- 1 tbsp olive oil
- 1 pound beef stew meat
- 2 oz curry paste
- 1 tbsp brown sugar
- 15 oz coconut milk
- ¼ cup beef broth or water
- 2 large potatoes, peeled and cut in cubes
- 1 onion, slices
- 2 tbsp roasted peanuts

Prep Time	10 Min.
Cooking Time	30 Min.
Smoking Time	5-10 Min.
Portion	2
Category	MAIN

INSTRUCTIONS

- Heat the olive oil in a pan on high heat and brown the beef from all sides.
  Add the onions and curry paste. Fry for 3 minutes.

- Add the coconut milk and bring to a boil.
  Reduce the heat and add the sugar, beef broth and potatoes.

- Transfer the mixture into a high pressure cooker and cook for 30 minutes until the meat is tender.

- Transfer the beef curry to plates and cover with a lid and place the hose of the smoking gun under it.
  Fill the smoking chamber with tthe cherry wood chips.
  Turn on the smoking gun and light the chips.
  Fill the bowl with smoke and remove the hose, keeping the lid on.
  Infuse the beef curry with the smoke for at least 5-10 minutes.

- Remove the lid.

- Serve the smoked beef curry with the roasted peanuts!

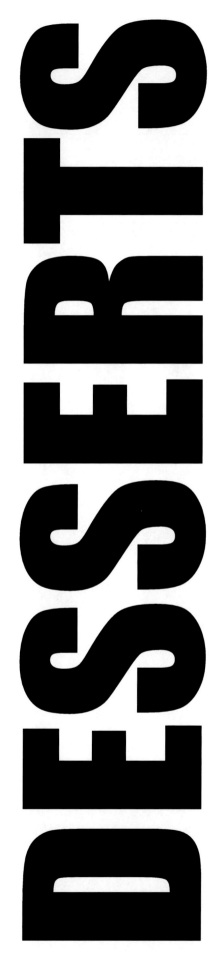

DESSERTS

SMOKED YOGURT WITH BERRIES

INGREDIENTS

- 2 cup greek yogurt
- 1 tbsp honey
- 1 tsp vanilla aroma
- ½ cup strawberries
- ½ cup blueberries
- ¼ cup cereals of your choice
- apple wood chips

Prep Time	5 Min.
Smoking Time	5-10 Min.
Portion	2
Category	DESSERT

INSTRUCTIONS

- In a large mixing bowl combine the yogurt with the honey.

- Cover the yogurt with a lid and place the hose under the lid.
  Fill the smoking chamber with the apple wood chips.
  Turn on the smoking gun and light the chips.
  Fill the bowl with smoke and remove the hose, keeping the lid on.
  Infuse the yogurt with the smoke for at least 5-10 minutes.
  Remove the lid.

- Transfer the yogurt to plates or bowls and garnish with the mixed berries and cereals of your choice!

SMOKED STRAWBERRY CRUMBLE

INGREDIENTS

- 1 lbs strawberries
- 1 tbsp cornstarch
- 2 tbsp sugar
- 1 tbsp lemon juice
- ½ cup all purpose flour
- ½ cup old fashioned oats
- ¼ cup brown sugar
- ½ tbsp vanilla extract
- ½ tsp cinnamon powder
- ¼ cup butter, melted
- cherry wood chips

Prep Time	10 Min.
Baking Time	25 Min.
Smoking Time	3-5 Min.
Portion	4
Category	DESSERT

INSTRUCTIONS

Preheat the oven to 320 °F. Dice the strawberries and sprinkle with the cornstarch. Mix well.

Add the sugar and lemon juice and mix well. Place the strawberries into a baking dish.

In a small bowl combine the oats, flour, brown sugar, vanilla, cinnamon powder and melted butter. Stir all with a fork until it crumbles.

Cover the crumbles with plastic wrap and place the hose under the plastic wrap. Fill the smoking chamber with the cherry wood chips. Turn on the smoking gun and light the chips. Fill the bowl with smoke and remove the hose, keeping the plastic wrap on. Infuse the crumbles with the smoke for at least 3-5 minutes. Remove the lid.

Place the crumbles over the strawberries and bake in the oven for 25 minutes until the crumbles turn light brown.

SMOKED STRAWBERRY CHEESECAKE

INGREDIENTS

- 4 cups cream cheese
- 1 cup sugar
- 1 cup whipping cream
- 1 tsp vanilla extract
- 2 cups graham crackers
- 6 tbsp butter, melted
- 2 cups Strawberries, diced
- 2 tbsp water
- 2 tbsp cornstarch
- ½ cup sugar

Prep Time	20 Min.
Smoking Time	5-10 Min.
Portion	1 Cake
Category	DESSERT

INSTRUCTIONS

- Crash the Graham crackers. Combine Graham crackers with the melted butter until incorporated.

- Place the cracker mixture in a bowl and cover with a lid. Place the hose under the lid. Fill the smoking chamber with the cotton wood chips. Turn on the smoking gun and light the chips. Fill the bowl with smoke and remove the hose, keeping the lid on. Infuse the cracker mixture with the smoke for at least 5-10 minutes. Remove the lid.

- Press the cracker mixture into a baking pan and chill in the fridge. Whisk the cream cheese with the sugar and vanilla extract until smooth. In a separate bowl, beat the cream until medium peak.

- Fold the whipped cream into the cream cheese mixture. Spread the filling over the cracker crust and chill in the fridge.

- Combine sugar, cornstarch, water and strawberries in a saucepan. Bring to a boil and stir for 10 minutes until the sauce has thickened. Top the cheesecake with the strawberry sauce in a thin layer. Let the cheesecake sit in the fridge.

- Serve the smoked strawberry cheesecake and top with some fresh strawberries!

SMOKED
RAISIN CUPCAKES

INGREDIENTS

- ½ cup raisins
- ½ cup butter, room temperature
- 1 cup white sugar
- 3 eggs
- 1 tsp vanilla extract
- 1 ½ cup flour
- 1 tsp baking powder
- pinch of salt
- ¼ cup milk

Prep Time	15 Min.
Baking Time	20 Min.
Smoking Time	3-5 Min.
Portion	10 Muffins
Category	DESSERT

INSTRUCTIONS

- Preheat your oven to 350 °F.

- In a bowl mix together flour, baking soda and salt.

- In another bowl, whisk the butter with the sugars until combined. Whisk in the eggs one by one.

- Add the flour, milk and vanilla extract. Add the raisins and stir.

- Fill cupcake liners with the batter and bake for 20 minutes. Place the Cupcakes on a cooling rack and cover with a lid. Place the hose under the lid. Fill the smoking chamber with the pear wood chips. Turn on the smoking gun and light the chips. Fill the bowl with smoke and remove the hose but keep the lid on. Infuse the cupcakes with the smoke for at least 3-5 minutes.

- Remove the lid.

- Serve the smoked raisin cupcakes and top with some additional raisins.

SMOKED PINEAPPLE DESSERT

INGREDIENTS

- ½ pineapple, trimmed and cut into thick slices
- ¼ cup dark rum
- 2 tbsp brown sugar
- 1 tbsp butter
- ¼ tsp ground cinnamon
- ½ cup mascarpone cheese
- 1 tbsp icing sugar
- ½ tsp vanilla aroma

Prep Time	15 Min.
Baking Time	20 Min.
Smoking Time	3-5 Min.
Portion	10 Muffins
Category	DESSERT

INSTRUCTIONS

- In a small bowl combine the mascarpone cheese with the icing sugar and vanilla extract.

- Mix well.

- In another bowl combine the rum with the sugar and mix until the sugar is dissolved.

- Place the pineapple slices on a baking dish and pour the rum mixture over the top. Coat the pineapple well with the mixture.

- Heat a pan on a medium high heat and brown the pineapple slices on both sides for 2 minutes. Add the butter and cinnamon.

- Cover the Pineapple slices with plastic wrap and place the hose under the plastic wrap. Fill the smoking chamber with the hickory wood chips. Turn on the smoking gun and light the chips. Fill the bowl with smoke and remove the hose, keeping the plastic wrap on. Infuse the crumbles with the smoke for at least 3-5 minutes.

- Remove the lid.

- Place the smoked Pineapple slices on a plate and top with the mascarpone cream.

SMOKED PECAN CHOCOLATE CAKE

INGREDIENTS

- ½ cup dark chocolate
- ½ unsalted butter
- 5 oz sugar
- 3 large eggs
- ½ tsp vanilla extract
- ¼ cup pecan nuts, chopped
- powdered sugar

Prep Time	10 Min.
Baking Time	30 Min.
Smoking Time	5-10 Min.
Portion	2
Category	DESSERT

INSTRUCTIONS

- Preheat the oven to 360 °F. Grease a baking pan and line with parchment paper.

- Melt the chocolate and butter in a microwave safe bowl until melted. Stir in the sugar and let the mixture cool down.

- Cover the chocolate with a lid and place the hose under the lid. Fill the smoking chamber with the apple wood chips. Turn on the smoking gun and light the chips. Fill the bowl with smoke and remove the hose, keeping the lid on. Infuse the chocolate with the smoke for at least 5-10 minutes.

- Remove the lid.

- Add the eggs to the chocolate, one at a time. Stir the mixture until it becomes thick. Stir in the vanilla extract and the pecan nuts.

- Pour the batter into the prepared pan and bake for 30 minutes.

- Let it cool in the pan, then take it out carefully.

- Dust with powdered Sugar and cut into wedges.

- Garnish with berries and pecan nuts.

SMOKED CHOCOLATE WAFFLES

INGREDIENTS

- 1 ½ cup flour
- 5 tbsp cornstarch
- 2 tbsp sugar
- 1 tbsp baking powder
- pinch of sea salt
- 1 cup whole milk
- 1 large egg
- 2 tbsp melted butter
- 1 tsp vanilla extract
- ½ cup dark chocolate

Prep Time	5 Min.
Baking Time	4 Min.
Smoking Time	3-5 Min.
Portion	4
Category	DESSERT

INSTRUCTIONS

- Preheat the waffle maker to high heat.

- In a large mixing bowl combine the flour, cornstarch, sugar, baking powder and salt. Mix well.

- Add the milk, eggs, melted butter and vanilla. Stir until smooth in texture.

- Pour some of the waffle batter into the hot waffle maker and cook for 4 minutes until cooked. Repeat with the remaining batter.

- Place the waffles on a plate and cover with a lid. Place the hose under the lid. Fill the smoking chamber with the apple wood chips. Turn on the smoking gun and light the chips. Fill the bowl with smoke and remove the hose but keep the lid on. Infuse the chocolate with the smoke for at least 3-5 minutes.

- Remove the lid.

- Garnish the pancakes with banana slices and honey. Serve!

SMOKED CHOCOLATE CHIP COOKIES

INGREDIENTS

• 1 cup butter, soft	**Prep Time** 20 Min.
• 1 cup sugar	**Baking Time** 30 Min.
• 1 cup brown sugar	**Smoking Time** 3-5 Min.
• 1 tsp vanilla extract	**Portion** 30 Cookies
• 2 large eggs	**Category** DESSERT
• 3 cups all purpose flour	
• 1 tsp baking soda	
• pinch of salt	
• 1 cup chocolate chips	
• cherry wood chips	

INSTRUCTIONS

Preheat your oven to 350 °F.

In a bowl mix together flour, baking soda and salt.

In another bowl, whisk the butter with the sugars until mixed. Add the eggs and vanilla extract, and whisk until fluffy. Mix in the dry ingredients, then add the chocolate chips.

Roll the dough into balls and place them on a pan lined with parchment paper. Bake for about 30 minutes in the oven until cooked.

Place the Cookies on a cooling rack and cover with a lid. Place the hose under the lid. Fill the smoking chamber with the cherry wood chips. Turn on the smoking gun and light the chips. Fill the bowl with smoke and remove the hose but keep the lid on. Infuse the cookies with the smoke for at least 3-5 minutes.

Remove the lid.

Serve the smoked cookies with a glass of milk!

SMOKED BANANA PANCAKES

INGREDIENTS

- 1 cup flour
- 1 tbsp sugar
- 2 tbsp butter
- 1 tbsp baking powder
- ¾ cup milk
- 1 large egg
- 1 banana, ripe
- 1 tbsp honey

Prep Time	5 Min.
Baking Time	10 Min.
Smoking Time	5-10 Min.
Portion	2
Category	DESSERT

INSTRUCTIONS

In a large mixing bowl, combine all Ingredients and whisk until smooth.

Heat a frying pan to the medium high heat.
Grease the pan and pour the pancake batter in the pan with a ladle.
Once the pancakes start to brown, flip them on the other side.

Remove from the pan and transfer to a plate.

Cover the pancakes with a lid and place the hose under the lid.
Fill the smoking chamber with apple wood chips.
Turn on the smoking gun and light the chips.
Fill the bowl with smoke and remove the hose, keeping the lid on.
Infuse the pancakes with the smoke for at least 5-10 minutes.
Remove the lid.

Garnish the pancakes with banana slices and honey. Serve!

SMOKED ALMOND BROWNIES

INGREDIENTS

- 2 eggs
- ¾ cup sugar
- 1 cup dark chocolate chips
- 6 oz coconut oil
- 2 tsp vanilla extract
- 2 tbsp milk
- ½ cup all purpose flour
- 1 tbsp cocoa powder
- ¼ tsp baking powder
- pinch of sea salt
- ½ cup almonds, sliced

Prep Time	5 Min.
Baking Time	30 Min.
Smoking Time	5-10 Min.
Portion	10 Brownies
Category	DESSERT

INSTRUCTIONS

- Preheat your oven to 360 °F.

- Melt the chocolate chips in the microwave. Meanwhile whisk together eggs, sugar, vanilla, milk and coconut oil. Add the melted chocolate to the mixture and whisk well.

- Add the dry Ingredients and mix well. Transfer the batter to a baking dish lined with parchment paper. Top with the sliced Almonds.

- Bake for about 30 minutes in the oven until cooked. Let it cool down, then slice into even squares.

- Place the Brownies on a plate and cover with a lid. Place the hose under the lid. Fill the smoking chamber with apple wood chips. Turn on the smoking gun and light the chips. Fill the bowl with smoke and remove the hose, keeping the lid on. Infuse the brownies with the smoke for at least 5-10 minutes.

- Remove the lid.

- Serve the brownies with additional almonds!

SMOKED CHOCOLATE MARBLE CAKE

INGREDIENTS

- 1 cup butter, softened
- 1 cup sugar
- 2 tsp vanilla extract
- 3 eggs, room temperature
- 2 cups cake flour
- 1 tsp baking powder
- pinch of salt
- ½ cup milk, room temperature
- cherry wood chips

Chocolate swirl
- 1 tbsp cocoa powder
- 1 tbsp milk

Prep Time	20 Min.
Baking Time	90 Min.
Smoking Time	5-10 Min.
Portion	8
Category	DESSERT

INSTRUCTIONS

🖐 Preheat the oven to 340 °F. Grease a loaf pan with some butter.

🖐 In a bowl, mix the butter, sugar and vanilla. Beat with an electric mixer for 2 minutes until the butter turns fluffy. Add the eggs and mix.

🖐 Add the flour, baking powder and salt, then mix on a low speed until the batter is creamy.

🖐 In a small bowl combine the cocoa powder and milk. Add the cocoa mixture to 1 cup of cake batter and stir by hand until combined.

🖐 Pour the cake batter into the prepared loaf pan and layer the vanilla batter and cocoa batter to get the swirl effect. Bake for 90 minutes until the cake is cooked inside. Place the marble cake on a plate and cover with a lid. Place the hose under the lid. Fill the smoking chamber with the cherry wood chips. Turn on the smoking gun and light the chips. Fill the bowl with smoke and remove the hose, keeping the lid on. Infuse the marble cake with the smoke for at least 5-10 minutes. Remove the lid.

🖐 Serve the marble cake with some extra chocolate sauce on the side. Enjoy!

SMOKED TOFU PUDDING

INGREDIENTS

- 1 gelatine sheet
- 1 cup soy milk
- 2 tbsp brown sugar
- ½ cup water
- 1 inch piece of ginger, thinly sliced
- pear wood chips

Prep Time	10 Min.	
Baking Time	10 Min.	
Smoking Time	2 Min.	
Portion	2	
Category	DESSERT	

INSTRUCTIONS

- Soak the gelatine sheet in a bowl with cold water for 10 minutes.

- Place the soy milk in a small pot and bring to a boil.
  Add the soaked gelatine and stir to dissolve completely.

- Remove the pot from the heat and pour into a container.
  Let sit in the refrigerator for 2 hours until set.

- Combine sugar and water in a pot and bring to a boil.
  Add the ginger slices and boil for 10 minutes.
  Cool down and set aside.
  Cut the pudding onto thin curds and place in serving bowls.

- Cover the pudding with a lid and place the hose of the smoking gun under it.
  Fill the smoking chamber with the pear wood chips.
  Turn on the smoking gun and light the chips.
  Fill the bowl with smoke and remove the hose, keeping the lid on. Infuse the tofu pudding with the smoke for at least 2 minutes.
  Remove the lid.

- Pour the cold ginger syrup over the curd and serve!

SMOKED CINNAMON CHURROS

Prep Time: 10 Min.   **Baking Time**: 20 Min.   **Smoking Time**: 3-5 Min.
Portion: 4   **Category**:   DESSERT

INGREDIENTS

- ½ cup water
- 1 tbsp butter
- 1 tbsp sugar
- ¼ tsp salt
- 2 eggs
- ½ tsp vanilla extract
- 1 cup oil for frying

Cinnamon Sugar

- 2 tbsp sugar
- 1 tsp cinnamon powder
- 4 strawberries
- cherry wood chips

INSTRUCTIONS

- In a pot mix water, butter, sugar and salt to a simmer. Add the flour and whisk until the mixture begins to form a ball. Cook on low for about 5 minutes.

- Set the mixture aside and allow to cool down.

- Add the eggs one by one until combined. Add the vanilla extract and mix well.

- Transfer the mixture to a piping bag with a star nozzle.

- In a heavy pot heat the oil for a deep fry to 270 °F. Carefully pipe the churros into the hot oil, about 5 inches long. Fry until the churros are golden brown. Transfer to a paper towel.

- Place the cinnamon sugar on a plate and cover with a lid. Place the hose under the lid. Fill the smoking chamber with the cherry wood chips. Turn on the smoking gun and light the chips. Fill the bowl with smoke and remove the hose, keeping the lid on. Infuse the sugar with the smoke for at least 3-5 minutes.

- Remove the lid.

- Toss the churros in the smoked cinnamon sugar. Serve the Churros with fresh Strawberries!

SMOKED COCONUT BANANA DESSERT

INGREDIENTS

- ½ lb ripe banana, sliced
- 3 tbsp sugar
- pinch of salt
- 1 tbsp small tapioca pearls
- 1 cup coconut milk
- ½ tsp white sesame seeds
- pear wood chips

Prep Time	5 Min.
Cooking Time	30 Min.
Smoking Time	3-7 Min.
Portion	2
Category	DESSERT

INSTRUCTIONS

Soak the tapioca pearls in warm water for about 20 minutes and drain.

Marinate the banana slices in the sugar for at least 30 minutes.

In a pot combine the bananas, coconut milk, tapioca and salt.
Simmer on medium high heat for 15 minutes until bananas are cooked.

Fill the bowls with the coconut dessert.
Cover with a lid and place the hose under the lid.
Fill the smoking chamber with the pear wood chips.
Turn on the smoking gun and light the chips.
Fill the bowl with smoke and remove the hose, keeping the lid on.
Infuse the coconut dessert with the smoke for at least 3-7 minutes.

Remove the lid.

Sprinkle some white sesame seeds on top of the bananas and serve chilled!

SMOKED CREPES SUZETTE

Prep Time: 10 Min.   **Cooking Time**: 5 Min.   **Smoking Time**: 3-5 Min.
Portion: 1   **Category**:   DESSERT

INGREDIENTS

- 1 ½ cups milk
- 2 eggs
- 1 cup flour
- 1 tbsp sunflower oil
- 2 tbsp butter
- pinch of salt
- 2 tbsp sugar

For the sauce
- 1 orange, pieces
- ½ cup
- ½ cup sugar
- 6 tbsp butter
- 2 tbsp orange liqueur

INSTRUCTIONS

- In a bowl combine milk, eggs, sunflower oil, salt and sugar.
  Slowly add the flour while mixing.

- Heat a large frying pan on high heat and add butter. Pour ¼ cup of batter into the pan and cook until the batter is cooked through from one side. Remove from the pan and set aside.

- Heat a sauce pan on medium high heat. Add sugar, butter, orange juice and liqueur. Bring to a boil then add the orange pieces and the crepes. Transfer the crepes to a plate.

- Cover the orange crepes with a lid or film and place the hose under it. Fill the smoking chamber with the pear wood chips. Turn on the smoking gun and light the chips. Fill the bowl with smoke and remove the hose, keeping the lid on. Infuse the orange crepes with the smoke for at least 3-5 minutes.

- Remove the lid.

- Serve the smoked crepes , topped with the orange sauce.

SMOKED EGG TARTS

INGREDIENTS

- 4 pastry tart shells
- ¼ cup cream
- ¼ cup sugar
- ½ cup whole milk
- 1 egg yolk
- 2 tsp cornstarch
- ½ tsp vanilla extract
- cherry wood chips

Prep Time	10 Min.
Cooking Time	20 Min.
Smoking Time	3-5 Min.
Portion	4
Category	DESSERT

INSTRUCTIONS

- For the custard, mix the cream, milk, sugar, egg yolk, cornstarch and vanilla extract in a saucepan until the sugar is dissolved.

- Place the mixture over low heat, whisking until it starts to thicken.

  When the custard is thick enough to coat a spoon, remove from the heat and continue to whisk. Set aside and cool completely.

- Preheat the oven to 320 °F.

  Fill the tart shells with the custard and place the pan in the oven.

  After 20 minutes of baking, check the tarts.

  When the surface of the custard is forming bubbles and getting brown, take them out of the oven and place on a cooling rack.

- Cover the tarts with a lid or film and place the hose under it.

  Fill the smoking chamber with the cherry wood chips, turn on the smoking gun and light the chips.

  Fill the bowl with smoke and remove the hose, keeping the lid on.

  Infuse the egg tarts with the smoke for at least 3-5 minutes.

- Remove the lid.

- Serve the smoked egg tarts warm! Enjoy!

SMOKED FRENCH TOAST

INGREDIENTS

- 3 cups french bread
- 2 tbsp butter
- 2 eggs
- ½ cup milk
- ¼ tsp cinnamon powder
- ½ tsp vanilla extract
- 1 tbsp brown sugar
- ¼ cup strawberries
- ¼ cup blueberries
- ½ tbsp icing sugar
- cherry wood chips

Prep Time	5 Min.
Cooking Time	30 Min.
Smoking Time	3-8 Min.
Portion	6
Category	DESSERT

INSTRUCTIONS

- Grease a casserole dish with the butter. Cut the french bread into cubes and add to the casserole.

- In a bowl combine milk, eggs, sugar, vanilla extract and cinnamon powder. Whisk the mixture until well combined and pour into the casserole.

- Wrap the casserole with film and place the hose under it.

  Fill the smoking chamber with the cherry wood chips.

  Turn on the smoking gun and light the chips.

  Fill the bowl with smoke and remove the hose, keeping the lid on.

  Infuse the french toast casserole with the smoke for at least 5-8 minutes.

- Remove the lid.

- Bake the french toast casserole in the oven for 30 minutes at 340 °F.

- Transfer the casserole onto a cooling rack and garnish with the strawberries and blueberries. Sprinkle the casserole with icing sugar and serve warm!

SMOKED ICE CREAM SANDWICH

INGREDIENTS

- 2 cups flour
- ⅔ cup cocoa powder
- pinch of salt
- ¾ tsp baking powder
- 0.75 cups butter, room temperature
- 1 cup sugar
- 1 egg, room temperature
- 1 tsp vanilla extract
- icing sugar for rolling
- ice cream of your choice
- cotton wood chips

Prep Time	5 Min.
Smoking Time	3-5 Min.
Portion	8
Category	DESSERT

INSTRUCTIONS

In a bowl combine the cocoa powder, flour, salt and baking powder. Set aside.

In a bowl mix together butter with sugar until fluffy. Add the egg and vanilla extract and mix well.

Add the dry ingredients to the wet ingredients and mix until a dough forms. Wrap the dough in parchment paper and place in the fridge for one hour.

Roll the dough of ¼ inch thickness in the icing sugar, then return to the fridge. Cut circles in the dough and place them on parchment paper. Place the cookies in a preheated oven at 375 °F for 10 minutes.

Remove from the oven and let them cool down on a cooling rack.

Cover the cookes with a lid or film and place the hose under it. Fill the smoking chamber with the cotton wood chips. Turn on the smoking gun and light the chips. Fill the bowl with smoke and remove the hose, keeping the lid on. Infuse the cookies with the smoke for at least 3-5 minutes. Remove the lid.

Scoop your favorite ice cream on the flat side of one cookie and top another cookie. Serve while frozen!

SMOKED RASPBERRY TART

INGREDIENTS

For the crust

- 4 frozen tart shells
- 1 cup fresh raspberries
- 1 lime, zest and juice
- ½ cup heavy cream
- 8 oz cream cheese
- pear wood chips

Prep Time	5 Min.
Chilling Time	60 Min.
Smoking Time	3-5 Min.
Portion	2
Category	DESSERT

INSTRUCTIONS

In a large bowl, beat the heavy cream until soft. Set aside.

In a separate whisk beat the cream cheese until soft and add the lime juice and zest.

Fold in the whipped cream.

Chill the mousse for at least 1 hour in the fridge.

Cover the lime mousse with a lid or film and place the hose under it.
Fill the smoking chamber with the pear wood chips.
Turn on the smoking gun and light the chips.
Fill the bowl with smoke and remove the hose, keeping the lid on.
Infuse the mousse with the smoke for at least 3-5 minutes.

Remove the lid.

Pipe the mousse into the tart shells and top with fresh raspberries and lime zest.

Serve chilled.

SMOKED RASPBERRY TRIFLE

INGREDIENTS

For the crust

- 2 cups raspberries
- 1 tbsp sugar
- 16 oz mascarpone cheese
- ¾ cup icing sugar
- 1 cup amaretto cookies
- 1 tsp almond extract
- cotton wood chips

Prep Time	15 Min.
Smoking Time	3-5 Min.
Portion	6
Category	DESSERT

INSTRUCTIONS

- In a bowl combine the mascarpone cheese, icing sugar and almond extract. Whisk the mixture until smooth and set aside.

- In a saucepan combine 1 cup of raspberries with the sugar. Boil the mixture on medium high heat until it thickens to a sauce. Set aside.

- Portion the mascarpone creme into 6 dessert glasses, then add a layer of the raspberry sauce on top.

- Cover the raspberry dessert with a lid or film and place the hose under it.

  Fill the smoking chamber with the cotton wood chips.

  Turn on the smoking gun and light the chips.

  Fill the bowl with smoke and remove the hose, keeping the lid on.

  Infuse the raspberry dessert with the smoke for at least 3-5 minutes.

- Remove the lid.

- Serve the smoked raspberry trifle chilled, topped with some fresh raspberries and amaretto cookies.

SMOKED SOUTHERN FRIED APPLES

INGREDIENTS

- 4 granny smith apples
- ½ cup butter, unsalted
- ½ cup sugar
- 1 ½ tsp cinnamon powder
- ¼ tsp vanilla extract
- ½ cup mascarpone cheese
- 1 tbsp sour cream
- ½ lemon, zest
- apple wood chips

Prep Time	5 Min.
Cooking Time	5 Min.
Smoking Time	3-5 Min.
Portion	6
Category	DESSERT

INSTRUCTIONS

Peel and cut the apples in wedges. Set aside.

Heat a frying pan on medium high heat, then add the butter.

Whisk in the sugar and cinnamon.

Add the apples and cook for about 5 minutes until softened.
For the mascarpone cream, combine the mascarpone cheese, sour cream and vanilla extract in a bowl and mix well.

Add the zest of lemon and transfer the cream in a bowl.

Cover the bowl with a lid or film and place the hose under it.
Fill the smoking chamber with the apple wood chips.
Turn on the smoking gun and light the chips.
Fill the bowl with smoke and remove the hose, keeping the lid on.
Infuse the mascarpone cream with the smoke for at least 3-5 minutes.
Remove the lid.

Serve the smoked mascarpone cream on top of the fried warm apples. Enjoy!

SMOKED STRAWBERRY MOUSSE

INGREDIENTS

- 1 pound fresh strawberries
- ⅔ cup fine sugar
- 10 oz whipping cream
- 2 fresh strawberries for garnish
- mint leaves
- hickory wood chips

Prep Time	10 Min.
Smoking Time	5 Min.
Portion	2
Category	DESSERT

INSTRUCTIONS

✼ Slice the strawberries in half.

Add the strawberries with the sugar in a blender and mix until smooth.

✼ In a bowl whisk the whipping cream until stiff peaks form.

Gently fold in half of the strawberry puree until the mixture forms a mousse.

✼ Divide the remaining strawberry puree into the bottom of 2 large glasses and top with the strawberry mousse.

✼ Cover the glasses with a lid and place the hose of the smoking gun under it.

Fill the smoking chamber with the hickory wood chips.

Turn on the smoking gun and light the chips.

Fill the bowl with smoke and remove the hose but keep the lid on.

Infuse the strawberry mousse with the smoke for at least 5 minutes.

✼ Remove the lid.

✼ Serve the smoked strawberry mousse with some more sliced strawberries and mint leaves. Enjoy chilled!

SMOKED SMOOTHIE BOWL

INGREDIENTS

- 6 strawberries, sliced
- 1 orange, sliced
- 1 red apple, sliced
- 10 oz frozen fruits
- 1 banana
- 5 tbsp almond milk
- ¼ tsp vanilla extract
- 1 tbsp honey
- 2 tbsp cereals
- pear wood chips

Prep Time	5 Min.	
Smoking Time	5 Min.	
Portion	2	
Category	DESSERT	

INSTRUCTIONS

In a blender combine the frozen fruits, banana, almond milk, vanilla extract and honey.

Blend on high for 1 minute until the mixture is smooth and thick.

Serve the smoothies into bowls and cover with a lid.

Place the hose of the smoking gun under it.
Fill the smoking chamber with the pear wood chips.
Turn on the smoking gun and light the chips.
Fill the bowl with smoke and remove the hose, keeping the lid on.
Infuse the smoothie bowls with the smoke for at least 5 minutes.

Remove the lid.

Serve the smoked smoothie bowls with sliced fruits and the granola. Enjoy!

SMOKED RICE PUDDING WITH MANGO

INGREDIENTS

- 1 cup short grain rice
- 3 cups milk
- 1 cup cream
- ¼ cup vanilla sugar
- pinch of salt
- orange peel
- 1 Mango, diced
- 1 Passionfruit
- cotton wood chips

Prep Time	5 Min.
Cooking Time	20 Min.
Smoking Time	4 Min.
Portion	4
Category	DESSERT

INSTRUCTIONS

⚜ In a pot combine the milk, cream, vanilla sugar, salt and orange peel.

Bring to a boil then add the short grain rice.

Boil the mixture again, then cover with a lid and boil for about 20 minutes until the rice is soft and the texture creamy.

⚜ Transfer the rice pudding to a plate.

⚜ Cover the rice pudding with a lid and place the hose of the smoking gun under it.

⚜ Fill the smoking chamber with the cotton wood chips.

Turn on the smoking gun and light the chips.

Fill the bowl with smoke and remove the hose, keeping the lid on.

Infuse the rice pudding with the smoke for at least 4 minutes.

⚜ Remove the lid.

⚜ Serve the smoked rice pudding warm with the diced mango and passionfruit. Enjoy!

SMOKED PASSIONFRUIT MOUSSE

INGREDIENTS

- 1 cup passionfruit juice
- ½ cup heavy cream
- 1 gelatine sheet
- 8 oz condensed milk
- ½ tbsp sugar
- 2 fresh passion fruits
- cotton wood chips

Prep Time	5 Min.
Chill Time	4 Hrs.
Smoking Time	5 Min.
Portion	6
Category	DESSERT

INSTRUCTIONS

In a small bowl with cold water, soak the gelatine for 10 minutes and set aside.

Bring the cream to a boil then add the soaked gelatine and mix well.
Let the cream cool down.

In a bowl combine the passion fruit juice, cream, sugar and condensed milk.
Pour the mixture into glasses and refrigerate for at least 4 hours.

Cover the passion fruit mousse with a lid and place the hose of the smoking gun under it.
Fill the smoking chamber with the cotton wood chips.
Turn on the smoking gun and light the chips.
Fill the bowl with smoke and remove the hose, keeping the lid on.
Infuse the passion fruit mousse with the smoke for at least 5 minutes.

Remove the lid.

Serve the smoked passion fruit mousse with fresh passion fruit pulp.

COCKTAILS

SMOKED CLASSIC MOJITO

INGREDIENTS

- 2 tbsp simple syrup
- fresh mint leaves
- ½ lime
- 1 cup ice cubes
- 2 oz white rum
- club soda
- pear wood chips

Prep Time		5 Min.
Smoking Time		30 Sec.
Portion		2
Category		COCKTAIL

INSTRUCTIONS

⚜ Place fresh mint leaves and 1 lime wedge into a glass.

With a muddler, crush the mint and lime to release flavor.

⚜ Add 1 more lime wedge and the simple syrup and mix well.

Fill the glass with ice cubes, then pour the rum over it.

Top with the club soda.

⚜ Place the drink smoker on top of the glass.

Load the smoking gun with pear wood chips and connect the hose to the drink smoker. Turn on the gun and fill with smoke.

Turn off the gun and let it infuse for 30 seconds.

⚜ Garnish with fresh mint leaves and lime wedges. Enjoy!

SMOKED CUCUMBER & GIN

INGREDIENTS

- 2 oz cucumber juice
- 2 oz gin
- 1 oz fresh lime juice
- 1 oz simple syrup
- cucumber slices, for garnish
- mint leaves, for garnish
- apple wood chips
- Ice cubes, crushed

Prep Time	5 Min.
Smoking Time	1 Min.
Portion	1
Category	COCKTAIL

INSTRUCTIONS

- In a cocktail shaker filled with Ice add the cucumber juice, gin, lime juice and simple syrup.

- Shake well until everything is combined and chilled.

- Pour into glasses filled with ice and place the drink smoker on top of the glass.

  Load the smoking gun with apple wood chips and connect the hose to the drink smoker.

  Turn on the gun and fill with smoke.

  Turn off the gun and let it infuse for 1 minute.

- Garnish with cucumber slices and fresh mint leaves. Enjoy!

SMOKED ORANGE NEGRONI

INGREDIENTS

- 1 oz Campari
- 1 oz Gin
- 1 oz red vermouth
- orange peel
- 2 dehydrated orange slices
- cherry wood chips

Prep Time		2 Min.
Smoking Time		1 Min.
Portion		1
Category		COCKTAIL

INSTRUCTIONS

⚜ In a cocktail shaker combine the Camparin, gin and vermouth.
Add some ice cubes then shake until the mixture is chilled.

⚜ Fill a glass with ice then strain the cocktail over the ice.

⚜ Place the drink smoker on top of the glass.
Load the smoking gun with cherry wood chips and connect the hose to the drink smoker.
Turn on the gun and fill with smoke.
Turn off the gun and let it infuse for 1 minute.

⚜ Garnish with the orange peels and dehydrated orange slices. Enjoy!

SMOKED PASSION FRUIT MARGARITA

INGREDIENTS

- 1 cup tequila
- ½ cup grand marnier
- ½ cup passion fruit puree
- 1 tbsp lime juice
- 1 tbsp sugar syrup
- 1 tbsp mild chili pepper powder
- 1 tbsp fine salt
- Ice cubes
- 2 dehydrated lime slices

Prep Time	5 Min.
Smoking Time	1 Min.
Portion	2
Category	COCKTAIL

INSTRUCTIONS

- In a small bowl combine the chili pepper powder and salt.

  Dip the rim of the glass in water then dip into the chili-salt mixture.

- In a cocktail shaker combine tequila, grand marnier, passion fruit, lime juice and sugar syrup and shake with some ice cubes.

- Strain the mixture into a glass with ice cubes and place the drink smoker on top of the glass.

  Load the smoking gun with wood chips and connect the hose to the drink smoker. Turn on the gun and fill with smoke.

  Turn off the gun and let it infuse for 1 minute.

- Garnish with dehydrated lime slices and enjoy!

SMOKED PINEAPPLE PUNCH

INGREDIENTS

- 1 small whole fresh pineapple, peeled and diced
- ½ tbsp sugar
- 2 tbsp lime juice
- 1 sprig mint leaves
- ½ cup white rum
- cotton wood chips

Prep Time	4 Min.
Smoking Time	2 Min.
Portion	2
Category	COCKTAIL

INSTRUCTIONS

- In a cocktail shaker combine the lime juice, mint leaves and rum.
  Shake well until combined.

- In a blender add the pineapple dices and the sugar.
  Blend it until smooth.

- Add the pineapple juice to the shaker and shake again until all is combined.

- Pour the mixture into glasses filled with ice and place the drink smoker on top of the glass.
  Load the smoking gun with cotton wood chips and connect the hose to the drink smoker.
  Turn on the gun and fill with smoke.
  Turn off the gun and let it infuse for 2 minutes.

- Garnish the smoked pineapple punch with fresh mint sprig and pineapple slices. Enjoy!

SEARCH CODES

Aioli, 5, 101

Almond, 4, 5, 37, 39, 139, 159, 165

Apples, 5, 161

Asparagus, 4, 33

Avocado, 4, 63

Bagel, 4, 59

Banana, 5, 133, 137, 147, 165

Basil, 4, 27, 29, 57, 99

Beef, 5, 81, 87, 97, 117

Berries, 5, 121, 123, 125, 131

Brie, 4, 37

Broccoli, 4, 5, 55, 87

Brownies, 5, 139

Butter, 4, 5, 25, 43, 45, 51, 55, 71, 81, 87, 93, 103, 105, 107, 111, 123, 125, 127, 129, 131, 133, 135, 137, 141, 145, 149, 153, 155, 161

Cake, 5, 125, 131, 141

Caprese, 4, 27

Cheese, 4, 5, 29, 33, 37, 41, 49, 53, 61, 71, 73, 79, 91, 93, 97, 107, 109, 125, 129, 157, 159, 161

Cheesecake, 5, 125

Chicken, 4, 5, 35, 41, 69, 85, 95, 105, 115

Chocolate, 5, 131, 133, 135, 139, 141

Churros, 5, 145

Cinnamon, 5, 39, 123, 129, 145, 153, 161

Corn, 4, 43

Crackers, 4, 53, 125

Crepes, 5, 149

Crumble, 5, 109, 123, 129

Cucumber, 5, 21, 23, 31, 53, 59, 61, 63, 69, 95, 109, 175

Cupcake, 5, 127

Curry, 5, 117

Egg, 5, 21, 39, 47, 65, 81, 95, 97, 113, 127, 131, 133, 135, 137, 139, 141, 145, 149, 151, 153, 155

Falafel, 4, 31

Garlic, 4, 17, 19, 29, 31, 33, 41, 45, 47, 55, 57, 65, 69, 71, 75, 77, 85, 87, 89, 91, 93, 95, 99, 101, 105, 107, 113

Gin, 5, 175, 177

Gnocchi, 5, 93

Hamburger, 5, 81

Ice Cream 5, 155

Mango 5, 167

Margarita, 5, 179

Meatball, 5, 65, 97, 99

Mojito, 5, 173

Mousse, 5, 157, 163, 169

Mozzarella, 4, 27, 41, 47, 49, 71, 79, 97, 107

Negroni, 5, 177

Orange, 5, 149, 165, 167, 177

Pancakes, 5, 133, 137

Parmesan 5, 29, 33, 71, 91, 93, 95, 97, 99, 111

Passionfruit, 5, 167, 169

Pasta, 5, 97, 99, 109

Pecan, 5, 29, 35, 39, 81, 83, 85, 95, 105, 131

Pesto, 4, 29

Pineapple, 5, 129, 181

Pinsa, 5, 79

Pitas, 5, 113

Pizza, 4, 49, 79

Popcorn, 4, 51

Pork, 4, 5, 13, 65, 77, 97, 111

Portobello, 5, 107

Potato, 4, 17, 25, 77, 93, 117

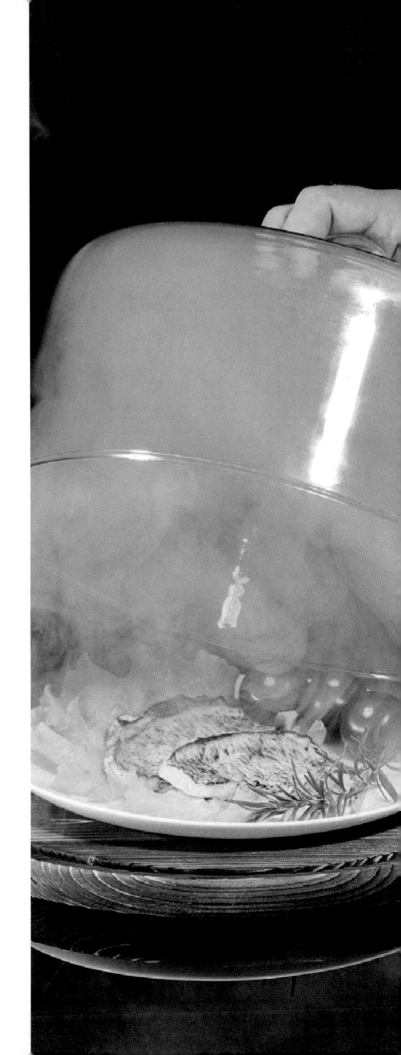

Made in the USA
Monee, IL
23 December 2023

bf9b652b-b2ac-4174-9fe5-059daddf0de5R01